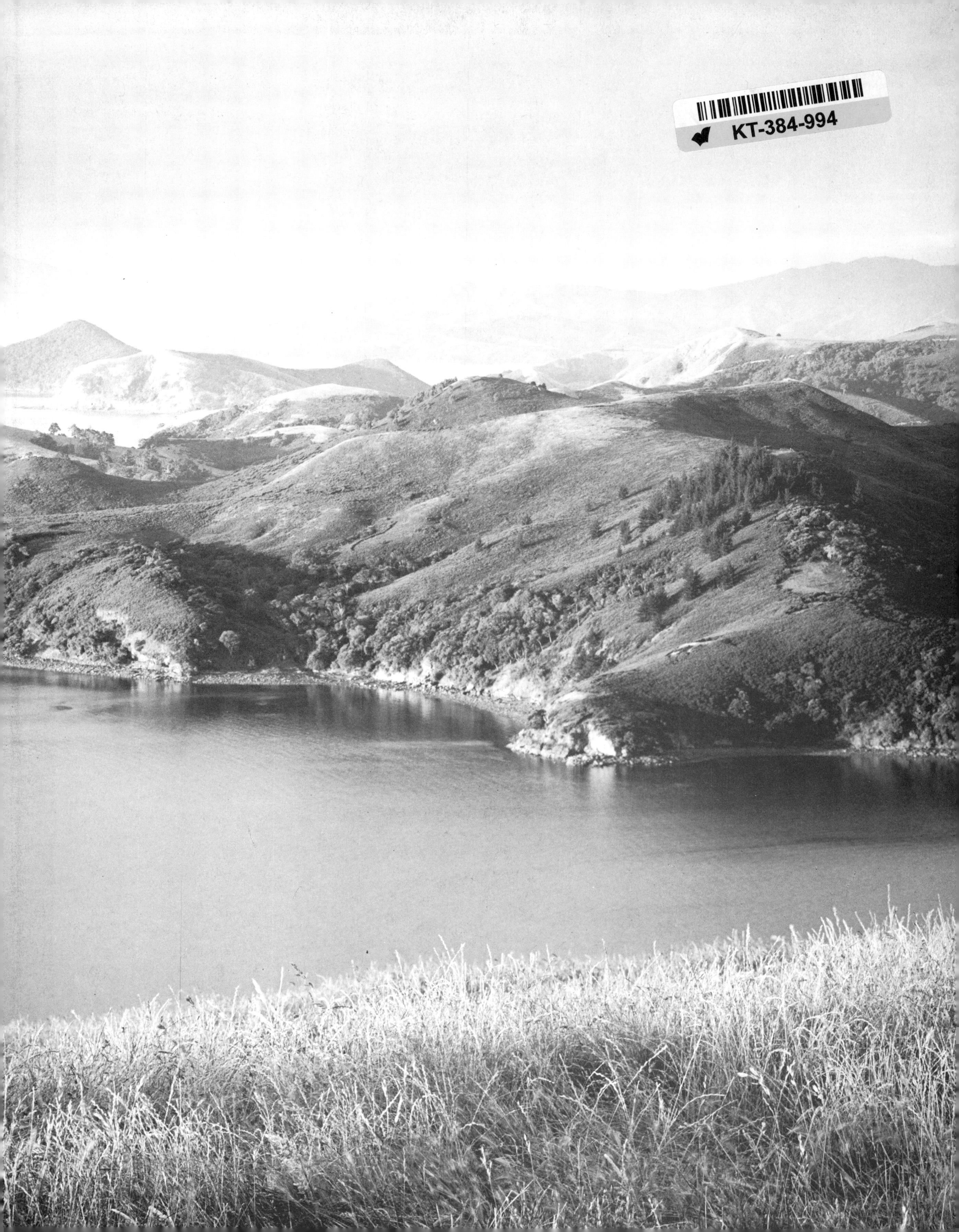

NEW ZEALAND

NEW ZEALAND

A CELEBRATION

Robin Bromby · Robin Smith · Warren Jacobs

CURREY O'NEIL

Acknowledgements
The Publisher wishes to thank Sir Charles Fleming and Mr Peter Johnson and the Department of Lands and Survey, New Zealand, for providing many of the pictures in the section on the outlying islands. Photographs supplied by this department appear on pages 66/67, 68 (above and below), 72, 73 (above and below), 74 and 75. The photograph on page 76 was reproduced with the permission of Mr Peter Johnson. Photographs on pages 65 and 68 (middle) were reproduced courtesy of Peter Harper. Photographs on pages 55 (bottom), 69, 70 and 71 are by John Warham Ph.D., FRPS. Thanks are also due to Mr Rollo Hammet of Melbourne, for supplying historical pictures from his library.

Published by Currey O'Neil Ross Pty Ltd
56 Claremont Street, South Yarra
Victoria 3141
First published 1984
© Photographs Robin Smith and Warren Jacobs
© Text Robin Bromby

ISBN 0 85902 090 8

Contents

1. The Farthest Paradise

No part of New Zealand is more than 110 kilometres from the sea. In this long, thin group of mountainous islands, roughly the same size as Britain or Japan in land area, live a mere 3.5 million people.

It is a country where there is a surprise around almost every corner. While the traveller's most enduring memory is the hundreds of square miles of lush pasture and the millions of sheep, it is harder for the mind to imagine the grandeur of the Southern Alps or the menace of the rocky coastline; each time one sees the vertical stone cliffs of the southern fiords and their rushing snow-fed rivers, it is a fresh impact which makes one gasp.

New Zealand is several countries in one. The southern fiords could be Norway, the mountains Austria, the cathedral city of Christchurch a piece of England transported to the other side of the world; in the barren, rocky hills of Central Otago, you could just as well imagine yourself to be in the Scottish Highlands, and the seemingly endless rows of planted pine forests of the North Island offer the illusion that this could be North America. Yet they all exist cheek-by-jowl, and the visitor can see it all within a few days.

The people can be just as surprising. There are, of course, the obvious differences between the European settlers of the last 140 years – the *pakehas* – and those who preceded them by several centuries, the brown-skinned Maori people, and the widespread intermarriage which has made New Zealand one of the more comfortable multi-racial countries in which to live. But within the *pakeha* population itself, the absence of any regional accents belies the subtle differences. The Scottish settlers of Dunedin (itself the ancient Celtic name for Edinburgh) and the English artisans who founded Christchurch have created a style of life that, under the surface, is to those people far removed from the aggressive, even hedonistic, get-rich-quick impulses which drive the country's largest city, Auckland, and its aspiring satellite of Hamilton.

For all the concentration of population in the four major cities, New Zealand is a country where one can quickly find peace and solitude. Within an hour's drive from any of the large cities, you can be driving along country highways, quite likely not seeing another car for several kilometres. The absence of very much heavy industry has left the air fresh and crisp, the rivers clean. By world standards, the cities are safe – and the police carry no guns.

Map of New Zealand and the outlying islands to the south and south east. (See page 61 for a map showing the Kermadec group of islands to the north.)

Page 9
The Southern Alps and the Tasman Sea.

Pages 10/11
Russell, Bay of Islands.
Russell, on the Bay of Islands, is a small peaceful town set amidst languid waterways. In its earliest days it was known as the "hell-hole of the Pacific" due to it being the main settlement of the white settlers, with grog shanties, violence and clashes with the local Maori part of its everyday life. This now quiet town is an important big-game fishing centre, while the less adventurous can find any number of launch trips around the picturesque bays.

Page 12
Milford Sound and Mitre Peak.
Milford Sound and the famed Mitre Peak, one of many fiords which indent this untamed part of New Zealand.

Page 13, above
Christchurch and Alps from Cashmere.
The people of the gracious South Island city of Christchurch live within an hour's drive of the ski fields. This superb view of the rich plains, part of the city and the mountains is taken from the hill suburb of Cashmere.

Page 13, below
Punakaiki Coast, looking north.
Punakaiki Coast, West Coast. It was near here that Abel Tasman first sighted New Zealand. Mariners since then, including Captain James Cook, have treated this coastline, with its often screaming winds and perilous currents, with the greatest of respect.

Pages 14/15
Wellington at night from Mount Victoria.
New Zealand's capital, Wellington, is built on hills surrounding a superb natural harbour. A drive around the hills, particularly to the top of Mount Victoria, provides spectacular views of the city.

Page 16
Fishing at the mouth of the Waitahanui River, Lake Taupo.
Lake Taupo, the country's largest lake, is one of the most popular inland fishing areas. The mouth of the Waitahanui River is the choicest spot on the lake, seen here at one of its less crowded moments. The quarry is trout, introduced into New Zealand last century and now maintained by a constant supply from a nearby hatchery.

Page 17
Steaming cliffs, Lake Rotomahana.
The steaming cliffs on Lake Rotomahana are one of the many reminders of the violence lying beneath the earth's thin crust in New Zealand's thermal region. It was here in 1886 that Mount Tarawera erupted, covering the famed Pink and White Terraces and bringing a horrific death to more than 150 people. Today the tourists slide by on boats and stare at the awesome wonder of the earth's forces.

Page 18, above
Matauwhai wharf, Bay of Islands.
The sea plays little part in the daily life of the modern New Zealander. Most of the small ships which originally plied the coast, going from port to port, have been superseded by road and air transport, so that now the sea is sailed for pleasure, as here at the Bay of Islands.

Page 18, below
Auckland city at night, from the north shore.
Auckland, the Queen City of New Zealand. It is the gateway to the nation, and as such has attracted a cosmopolitan population, the most recent of which are the large numbers of settlers from the South Pacific Islands.

Page 19
Sunrise, Queen Charlotte Sound, Picton.
Queen Charlotte Sound at sunrise. This deep sound, one of the vast enclosed waterways at the northern tip of the South Island, has traditionally offered safe anchorage. Captain James Cook sought refuge here on his voyages of discovery when he needed to repair and replenish his ships. Today the sound is a welcome sight, after the usually rough seas of Cook Strait, for the ferries that make their daily trips from Wellington.

Page 20
Pohutu geyser, Whakarewarewa.
Pohutu geyser, near Rotorua. At irregular intervals it springs into life, sending hundreds of litres of water to heights of more than thirty metres.

Health care is relatively free, and comprehensive accident and superannuation programmes are the most recent buttresses for what was already a comprehensive welfare state.

The public demand for and acceptance of such a cushion of welfarism is hardly surprising. Those born into post-war generations have known relative comfort, even luxury by world standards, most of their lives. The golden 1950s, with the wool price boom of the Korean War, was a period of full employment and there was a feeling that this was "God's Own Country". New Zealand is now facing grave economic problems, but even the 1960s and 1970s saw no real fall in the living standard. In its short history, New Zealand has been through many tough and difficult times, and in the depressions of the 1880s and the 1930s the great bulk of the population suffered from privation and distress just as much as did any other people of the Western world. The country had hardly got going when the first blow fell, just thirty-nine years after the first organised settlers arrived. The depression of 1879–1896 was so fierce, so long-lasting, in its misery and travail, that it created the public cry for something better – and the welfare state was founded, and in 1898 the first old age pension law was enacted by the Parliament. The prosperity of the early years of the century was short-lived. By 1921, with the post World War I boom expended, men were again walking off their farms. Although the economy did recover, and public fortunes fluctuated, it was a time of uncertainty and some fear – "Utopia Unrealised", as one historian has termed it – and, with the 1930s approaching, the fear was justified. The Great Depression scarred a whole generation, and left a legacy which has not even yet been extinguished from the minds of those who lived through it.

Yet for all the troubles which the country and its people have faced, the visitor from larger, more impersonal cities and nations notices immediately the easy-going, friendly and helpful nature of the people. But they are also for the most part resourceful, hard-working and hardy. They have to be. New Zealand is a land which is a challenge to man. More than three-quarters of the land area is over 200 metres above sea level, and hills and mountains abound. Being on a major fault line and with many volcanic and geothermal areas, the country has seen its share of major disasters. Over the last two decades, millions of dollars have been poured into rebuilding much of the central part of the capital city. Wellington has a reputation for sharp earthquakes, and there has been a great amount of concern about the ability of the old buildings to withstand a major quake. After all, the first settlers of Wellington had many of their homes destroyed by earthquake in 1848; the first intimations of the instability of the land on which they had settled were a series of tremors within the early months of 1840, when the first shiploads of settlers had barely settled in. Again, in 1855, more than a dozen Maori and Europeans were killed by an earthquake which struck near Wellington. In 1929, the small South Island township of Murchison was practically destroyed by a massive earth movement felt throughout the country; only seventeen people were killed in that first shock, but the quakes continued for two weeks, destroying roads, railways and bridges and permanently altering the landscape. Two years later, the greatest disaster in New Zealand's history took the form of the Hawke's Bay Earthquake. More than 250 people died, not only in the massive shock which swallowed most of Bluff Hill and turned a lagoon into a dry plain, destroying most of the city of Napier, as well as demolishing large sections of the nearby town of Hastings, but in the huge fires which swept both towns in the aftermath of the shocks. Disaster returned to the South Island in 1968 when Inangahua, just a short distance from Murchison, was struck by another horrific earthquake, although this time without the same loss of life as that which Murchison had suffered.

The living evidence of the geological ferment which has shaped New Zealand's mountains and valleys are the two volcanoes at the centre of the North Island – Ruapehu (2797 metres) and Ngauruhoe (2290 metres) – which still occasionally burst into life with eruptions of steam and ash. It was the discharge of water from the crater lake of Mt Ruapehu – a *lahar* – which caused the Tangiwai tragedy, when 151 holidaymakers died in appalling and terrifying circumstances on Christmas Eve, 1953. The sudden rush of water swept away the railway bridge over the Whangaehu River just before the Wellington to Auckland express was due to cross.

Around the central volcanic region, seismologists record more than a hundred earthquakes each year, most of them minor. North of the volcanoes is the famed tourist attraction of Rotorua, where the constant frenzy of the seismic activity has broken the earth's surface. In 1886, nearby Mt Tarawera erupted for six hours, killing 153 people in surrounding Maori villages and covering the fabulous Pink and White Terraces, by then considered one of the wonders of the world.

Today, the area is constantly overrun by tourists, as it is one of the top two or three items on the itinerary of foreign visitors. The rivers run with hot water, geysers hurl water metres into the air, and the Maori people show how they can cook in the hot pools alongside mudpools which bubble and gurgle. The thermal wonderland, an accurate description even though worn thin by a thousand travel brochures, is one of the many faces of New Zealand waiting for the visitor. Not that even Rotorua is overcrowded at the peak of the tourist season.

In the far north is the Bay of Islands, with its beautiful bays and tranquil waters, rich with the history of early New Zealand. It was here the first adventurers, who included certain missionaries, tried to buy land from the Maori, and where in 1840 Captain Hobson, acting for the British Government, persuaded the Maori chiefs to sign the Treaty of Waitangi by which they accepted the protection and rule of Queen Victoria.

Auckland, the largest of New Zealand's cities (population 825,000 – 56 per cent of the nation's population lives in the five major cities) is a multi-racial city. The last few decades have seen thousands of migrants from the Cook Islands and Niue, who carry

Queen Street Wharf, Auckland, in the 1880s. The founding of Auckland in 1840 encouraged settlers to come down from the Bay of Islands, many of them pioneer-tradesmen, and they quickly helped to build the stores which surround the flourishing port. In spite of labour shortages Auckland grew fast, and grew faster as boatloads of emigrants arrived from Scotland and England. Queen Street was to grow into an incredibly busy thoroughfare.

New Zealand passports even though their homes now have internal self-government, and Samoans whose homeland was a United Nations trustee territory under New Zealand administration. Add to these a not inconsiderable number of Tongans and other island people, they make with the Maori and *pakeha* New Zealander a fascinating human mixture. The city itself sits on a narrow stretch of land between two magnificent harbours – Manukau and Waitemata – and the suburbs are dotted with the mounds of extinct volcanoes. It is a busy, commercially important metropolis which, together with its surrounding dormitory and satellite towns, is growing at a cracking pace.

South of Auckland, apart from Rotorua, there is a rich variety of sights, from the eerie glow-worm caves at Waitomo to the Waikato River, harnessed at several points to produce hydro-electricity for the industrial north. Winding south by road through the hilly King Country, so named because it was the home of the Maori king who led his tribes against the European settlers in the Maori Wars of 1860–1872, it is possible to see the Maori people in their traditional country surroundings. In towns like Taumaranui and Te Kuiti, Maori institutions, including meeting houses and churches, are, if not dominant, at least indicative of the large Maori populations in the King Country. Unlike most other parts of the nation, much of the farming land in the King Country is still in Maori hands and farmed on the same scale and size as neighbouring *pakeha* holdings. It is in these rural strongholds that the Maori language, once thought in danger of becoming extinct, is still spoken, and indeed encouraged.

The central North Island contains many tourist attractions, from the skiing at Ruapehu, to trout fishing and boating on Lake Taupo, with less than a day's driving to the splendid beaches of the Bay of Plenty – named by Captain Cook for its prodigious supplies of food. Across the other side of the North Island is the dairy farming Taranaki province, dominated by the extinct volcano, Mt Egmont (2518 metres), compared in its conical shape to Japan's legendary Mt Fuji. Although most of Taranaki's forest has long been cleared for farming, much of the landscape retains a barely tamed appearance, with outcrops of bush and rolling hills, unlike the Hawke's Bay on the east coast, which has a more cultured landscape largely due to the widespread intensive farming, particularly orchards, although the province also contains some of the largest sheep farms in the country and the closest New Zealand has (along with some parts of the South Island) to a landed gentry.

At the southern tip of the North Island, is Wellington, the capital and administrative centre of the nation (population 342,000), a city set on a magnificent sheltered harbour and ringed by hills. With so little flat land available, the city's airport – the busiest in New Zealand – has been built out into Cook Strait in order to be able to take modern jet aircraft, even though it is still not capable of handling the larger jumbos now in service. Wellington, as noted earlier, has largely been rebuilt in the downtown business area. Once a city of two- and three-storey wooden

War canoe as seen from the *Endeavour* (after a drawing by Sydney Parkinson). The Maoris were expert sailors and built impressive war canoes that were up to seventy feet in length. These were powered by 100 men who kept time with long paddles, and sails of matting were sometimes erected when extra speed was required.

23

structures built along narrow commercial streets, barely wide enough in places for double tram tracks, it is now lined with rows of tall concrete buildings, with demolition of the old allowing much street widening, even if it has meant that the flavour and nature of the city has been irrevocably altered. It is still possible, however, to wander the inner suburban residential areas where the near impossible landscape produced ingenious methods of home construction. Narrow streets and alleys were lined with three-storey wooden homes (five-storey in some parts) which took a miniscule quantity of land area, and clung to the hills. The inner-city Wellingtonian spends a great deal of his or her life bent almost double, puffing and panting up steep streets and footpaths.

At the end of the 1850s, New Zealand had a European population of about 75,000 of which about 40,000 lived in the South Island. The absence of large numbers of Maoris had allowed settlement to proceed with less check, but the South's dominance, enhanced for a few more decades by the fortuitous discovery of gold both on the West Coast and in Otago, was eventually doomed once Maori resistance in the North was crushed, and the massive land grab could begin unhindered. Now 73 per cent of the country's total population lives north of Cook Strait.

While that stretch of water still provides a challenge to seamen travelling between the two islands, it takes only about twenty minutes to cross by air from the nearest major airport at Blenheim to Wellington. While the aeroplanes fly it in these brief minutes, storms blow up so quickly that it is not uncommon for the car ferries which cross the Strait to have their sailings cancelled – no one has forgotten that, in 1968 in one of those storms, the passenger ferry *Wahine* was wrecked with the loss of fifty-two lives.

Once over the Strait, though, Marlborough and Nelson, the two northernmost provinces in the South Island, bask in a reputation as two of the sunniest parts of New Zealand. Marlborough is best known for its fine-wooled sheep, and a fledgling wine industry; wine-growing was hitherto thought only possible in the much hotter north of the country. The province also has the Marlborough Sounds, whose complex pattern of bays and waterways and offshore islands are served only by boat. Nelson, one of the earliest settlements in the South Island, is best known for its orchards and tobacco growing.

From Nelson, the roads lead south to Westland, or the West Coast as it is more popularly known. The Coast is redolent with history, more so because its present is no more than a shadow of its former self. When gold was discovered in 1865, more than 15,000 miners came from Australia alone. Shanty towns sprang up, and today nary a signpost records where they stood. Those that did survive, albeit barely, such as Kumara which produced from a local miner and publican New Zealand's most colourful leader, Richard John Seddon, have been reduced today to a few lonely buildings.

The Coast is separated from the remainder of the country by the

Wellington, about 1875. Wellington, the capital of New Zealand since 1865, when the seat of government shifted from Auckland, is situated on the southern tip of the North Island, in the geographical centre of the country. Rimming Port Nicholson, an almost land-locked natural harbour, the business district restricts itself today to the low-lying areas, while the suburbs creep up into the surrounding hills where they enjoy sunny positions and expansive views of the harbour. Though the site was chosen in 1839, the first immigrants did not arrive until January 1840. This photograph of 1875 shows Wellington thirty-five years after settlement, and ten years after having become New Zealand's capital, marking the progress its founders had made in the first decades. (Alexander Turnbull Library, Wellington.)

Southern Alps, which form the backbone of the South Island. Mt Cook is the highest peak in New Zealand, at 3764 metres. The Alps, on a clear day, can be seen from either coast of the island and have always formed a fearsome barrier. Now, they provide the major skiing grounds, and aeroplanes on skis can take tourists into mountain areas that were once accessible only to the most intrepid mountaineers.

Sloping gently away to the east are the Canterbury Plains, the granary of New Zealand, which produce half the country's wheat, one-third of the threshed oats and more than half its barley, not to mention three-quarters of the nation's pea production. Competing for the land available are the sheep, because these fertile plains, neatly divided into paddocks, comprise one of the best areas for fat lambing ("Canterbury lamb" once being considered the ultimate in meat), while the uplands stretching into the foothills of the Alps are ideal for Merino wool growing. The plains are dissected by the great spread of fast flowing rivers – the Rakaia, Ashburton, Rangitata and Waimakariri. Thundering across the Rakaia in an express train, the echoes of the steel wheels on the steel bridge, the traveller expects to see the other bank after passing over gushing channels of green water, only to find that beyond the next peak of gravel there is yet another arm of this magnificent waterway.

Further south another great river, the Waitaki, provides a border between Canterbury and Otago. Otago's main city, Dunedin, was founded in 1848 by Scottish settlers and was a Presbyterian backwater until gold was discovered by Gabriel Read near what is now Lawrence. By 1863, two years after the discovery, Dunedin's population had exploded to 60,000, making it by far the largest town in the colony. While the gold soon went, and the miners with it, the residual benefits were great and Dunedin's economic boom lingered for decades. The legacy of those years is the collection of magnificent buildings, most of stone, which still exist. While Dunedin has been an economic backwater over the last twenty years, the lack of pressure for redevelopment has meant fewer threats of destruction to historic buildings than in most other cities. While some, like the Stock Exchange, were lost, the civic feeling in Dunedin has prevented any more recent demolitions; the people of Dunedin have a creditable record in preserving their architectural heritage, so that many fine examples of Victorian building not only survive but still fulfil their intended function.

Inland from Dunedin is Central Otago, quite unlike any other part of New Zealand. Nestling in the foothills of the Alps are the great lakes – Wanaka, Wakatipu and Hawea – all fed by water from the mountains, and the smaller but charmingly picturesque Lake Hayes. Otago, perhaps more than any part of New Zealand save the Bay of Islands, is redolent with the history of early European settlement. The tailings from gold diggings are to be found in many places; many stone cottages erected by miners or early farmers still exist either as recognisable shells or restored homes; towns such as Cromwell or Lawrence retain much of the look of towns a century ago. Central Otago has a low rainfall by New Zealand standards, with the result that part of the landscape consists of bare hills with imposing rock formations, or high hills with wind-swept tussock. The frosts and dry summer – which make it ideal for fruit growing (Central Otago apricots are famous throughout the country) – contrast with the bitterly cold winters and frequent heavy snow falls. Along the road between Roxburgh and Alexandra there stands a stone memorial at Gorge Creek, now a pretty gully with a picnic area, but once the mining canvas town of Chamounix Creek full of stores, hotels and pubs. In 1863, many miners were caught in a freak snow storm on their way across the Old Man Range to the latest gold find at Campbell's Diggings, and never made it down off the mountain.

Dunedin, Otago in the 1880s. The city of Dunedin, established in 1848, boomed in the 1860s to become the colony's largest town when gold was discovered in nearby Lawrence.

These days, it is a matter for complaint if the snow does not fall frequently and in quantity, because this is the home of Coronet Peak, regarded as one of the major skifields of the world, and in recent years there have been plans to build ski resorts on other slopes in Otago as more and more international visitors arrive for the winter season. Nearby to Coronet is the historic mining village of Arrowtown which, although now aimed full-blast at the tourist, still retains some of its old character, including a beautifully preserved row of miners' cottages. At the head of Lake Wakatipu is Queenstown, a thriving tourist centre with some of the greatest views from hotel windows in the southern hemisphere.

The province has many deserted towns and backwaters which fascinate those who are yearning for the atmosphere of history. From Arrowtown, one can walk up the banks of the Arrow River to Macetown, where a few remnants of miners' houses remain, and a huge quartz-crushing battery. Now it is a quiet little valley, where the vines and bushes have taken over once again. Standing there in the silence of a hot summer's day, it is difficult to imagine that once there was a thriving town of 3000 people.

The mountains and lakes – the silent and brooding Manapouri, and, nearby, Te Anau – lead into New Zealand's most remote region, Fiordland. Deep valleys of native forest divided by steep hills and mountains, seen only by the more adventurous trampers and the pilots of helicopters used for shooting the exotic deer, New Zealand's greatest pest. The rest of Southland province is very much more accessible, being one of the lushest pasture areas. Here the accent is on fat lambs and fodder crops, while the main city, Invercargill, is the southernmost city in the British Commonwealth; only one other settlement of any size lies at a lower latitude, Port Stanley in the Falklands.

Across the Foveaux Strait from Invercargill, a stretch of water which can be just as treacherous as the more northerly Cook Strait, lies Stewart Island, 1746 square kilometres but with a population of just over 500, practically all of whom live on the shores of Halfmoon Bay.

The bay is a suitable link with the Bay of Islands in the north. Not so large or impressive, certainly, but the other end of this paradise. Fishing boats ride at anchor; the main street parallels the beach, empty for most of the time except for customers at the post office or hotel, or when the steamer from Bluff arrives and the day-trippers and bush walkers pass through. The bush starts from the shore, and the most that can be seen of many of the houses is the roof. The only other anchorage of any note is near the southern tip, Port Pegasus. It was here that a fish-processing factory once stood, and before that miners worked a small and short-lived tin deposit. Now the bush has taken over again at Pegasus, and only fishermen ever get to visit this beautiful harbour of many bays and inlets.

Southwards lies the Antarctic, save for a few rocky outcrops. The Snares, Antipodes and the Bounty Islands are mere dots in the vast ocean, populated by seals and sea birds, while the southernmost is Campbell, once a sheep property, now a meteorological station. Only the Auckland Islands, 612 square kilometres, were ever settled on any scale, but that was a sad and dismal experiment. Now the Aucklands, like the other southern islands, are wildlife sanctuaries.

But, could it not be argued, how can New Zealand be considered a paradise? Does it not have present problems just like anywhere else? Of course. But, by the standards of the world today, this country has much that other peoples would envy. The standard of living is high, the cities are safe, the people are among the most polite and friendly in the world. The air is clean, the soil rich and fertile. Free education is available to all, no one is denied comprehensive health care, and the wide-reaching and generous welfare provisions eliminate the worst aspects of personal misfortune.

New Zealand is a comfortable paradise.

Queenstown, Otago, in the 1880s. Queenstown, on the shores of the lovely Lake Wakatipu, has the Southern Alps and the Remarkables towering above it. Probably the leading winter resort town of the South Pacific, Queenstown today services the nearby ski field of Coronet Peak as well as attracting visitors from neighbouring fields.

Page 29
Beech forest, Diamond Lake, Otago.
Beech forests once covered much of the South Island and important remnants provide vital cover for the slopes. Here a gravel track winds between the trees leaving the forest relatively undisturbed at Diamond Lake, Otago.

Pages 30/31
Wanganui River from Gentle Annie.
The Wanganui is one of New Zealand's major rivers. The Maori used it as an important canoe route to bypass the great forests on either side, and for many decades after European settlement it was used by a regular steamer service. Until quite recent times settlements up the river were isolated from many of the normal services available to communities.

Page 32
Lake Tarawera, Rotorua.
Lake Tarawera is seen here with the broken mountain Tarawera in the distance. On 10 June 1886 Tarawera exploded with devastating force, burying the little village of Te Wairoa and other lakeside settlements.

Page 33, above
Waikato River at Hamilton.
Hamilton city was built as two separate settlements on the Waikato River, once plied by trading vessels and gunboats. Rich tropical foliage borders the river minutes from the city centre.

Page 33, below
Rain forest on Mount Egmont.
New Zealand's climate, ranging from subarctic to subtropical, creates a great diversity of vegetation – including the magnificent rain forest on Mount Egmont.

Page 34, above
Cabbage-tree, Mahia Peninsula.
Sheep graze by a lone cabbage-tree on Mahia Peninsula at the northern tip of Hawke's Bay.

Page 34, below
Lake Hayes, autumn.
Lake Hayes is set in scenes of pastoral beauty and great splendour in autumn. The lake is so abundant in trout that the fishing season lasts from October until the end of August.

Page 35
Morning mist, Hikumutu.
A lasting impression on visitors from Europe and America are the long stretches of road with no other traffic. Here the early morning mist hangs over the silent road and countryside at Hikumutu.

Pages 36/37
Mount Egmont landscape.
The land flanking Mount Egmont's northern aspect was heavily forested a century ago. Today, while the rutted plains have been cleared, the mountain, now a popular ski field, still wears a dark mantle of forest on her slopes.

Page 38, above
Mount Ruapehu and crater lake.
Mount Ruapehu is the third of New Zealand's volcanoes, seen here with the crater lake which in 1953 drained suddenly into Whangaehu River. The huge wall of water and rock swept away the bridge which carried the Main Trunk Railway across the river. The Wellington-to-Auckland express was only minutes away and the engine and leading cars plunged into the river. In all, 151 people died in those few horrific moments.

Page 38, below
Hill pattern north of Lawrence, Otago.
Lawrence, near the first gold discoveries in New Zealand, has now reverted to a quiet farming area. In the 1920s and 1930s flowering daffodils covered many of the areas and excursion trains brought people from Dunedin to pick them. Today the railway has gone but the daffodils continue to bloom across the paddocks.

Page 39
Wairau Falls, Northland.

Page 40
Fox Glacier.
One of two major glaciers which make their way, centimetre by centimetre, down from the Southern Alps is Fox Glacier, nearly fourteen kilometres in total length. A few kilometres north is Franz Josef Glacier, a similarly impressive sight.

2. The Land

New Zealand's long thin shape, passing through several degrees of latitude, make it subject to a variety of climates, from subtropical in the far north, to a cold, temperate climate in the southern part of the South Island, with its southernmost island territories having a sub-Antarctic climate. By northern hemisphere standards, New Zealand should have a drier, warmer climate all over judging by its distance from the Equator. But the fact that its nearest continental neighbour – Australia – is 1500 kilometres away to the west, while there are 10,600 kilometres of ocean to the east between New Zealand and South America, makes for a different set of rules. The North Island is the same distance from the Equator as the Mediterranean Sea, with Auckland at the same latitude south as the sun-drenched Adriatic and Portugal are to the north, but temperatures on average are far lower in New Zealand due to the vast sea areas which surround it.

Being overall a temperate climate, seasonal variations are not very great. The northern part of the country is comfortable all year round, while even in the south – apart from the high country – winters have none of the ferocity of northern Europe. The weather is dominated by eastward-moving winds and depressions, and the high mountains in the South Island result in heavy rainfall on their westward side (Hokitika receives more than 3000 millimetres a year) while the Canterbury Plains and Central Otago have a comparatively light annual rainfall; the latter averages 330 millimetres a year.

The one factor which is common to most of the country is wind. "Windy Wellington" is the universally-known sobriquet for the capital city, and justly earned, with the wind able to stop a pedestrian in his tracks or, if he is particularly frail, knock him to the ground. The winds batter most of the country from time to time, and make the surrounding seas stormy and treacherous. Storms blow up quickly, and sometimes with little warning.

The temperate climate allowed, before the known arrival of man, the development of a luxuriant forest over most of the land, of which there are now only remnants. On the drier slopes of the North Island giant kauri trees grew, with the white pine kahikatea on the lower levels. On the West Coast of the South Island there was a rich variety of trees, tree-ferns and ground mosses, towered over by the beech forest. Other evergreens included the rimu and totara, while other trees produced magnificent flowers – the red of the pohutukawa, the yellow of the kowhai and the crimson of the rata. On the plains, probably Canterbury mostly, the giant moa – its wings no longer useful because, until the arrival of the Maori, it had no natural enemy and, hence, no need to resort to quick flight. So numerous were the types of birds even in the early years of European settlement, that the first settlers at Dunedin in 1848 reported that they could not sleep on the ships at anchor because of the cacophony coming from the forest on the nearby shores. The only mammals, apart from the native bat, were the thousands of seals, sea lions and sea elephants which came to the southern shores for the annual moult and mating seasons.

The first Polynesian settlers discovered a country which, prior to their arrival, had been physically separated from the rest of the world. The discovery of fossil remains suggests that there were twenty-seven types of moa, and four kiwi species, but how many of these were still in existance upon the landing of the Polynesians is not known, but supposed to be almost all. The largest of the moas was the *Dinornis maximus,* which stood more than three metres high, with huge – in terms of girth – legs, and would have consumed as much grass in a day as a cow, but they supplemented the grass with berries. Like the other moas, it was slow moving, certainly could not take to the air, and so was an obvious source of food for the human moa-hunter. The most popular prey was the *Euryapteryx,* which was about the same height as a man. By the end of the eighteenth century, it seems, the moa was extinct. Maori legend has it that when the chief Kupe first discovered the Land of the Long White Cloud, Aotearoa, other native birds were so unused to man that they could be taken by hand out of the trees.

The Great Fleet of canoes which established Maori settlement brought with it a variety of Polynesian plants, and particularly the kumara; this sweet potato, today still part of both the Maori and *pakeha* diet, dictated where the Maori settled. The greatest number of Maori settlements were in Northland, Auckland, Bay of Plenty, Poverty Bay, Nelson and Taranaki; not only were these places where the kumara thrived best, but they were among the warmer parts of the country – which suited a people used to the tropical islands of the Pacific – and apart from Nelson and Taranaki, were the parts of the land geographically most logical for migration from the north. The tribes which did later inhabit the colder and more southerly locations were generally those forced to do so either after being vanquished in battle, or in fear of that being the case. They lived mainly in coastal areas, and cleared as much forest as they needed for cultivation.

The damage that was done by the Maori was to the fauna rather than flora. Used to a diet which included pig and fowl on the islands whence they came, the new settlers had only the dogs and rats which they brought with them. So, they naturally turned to the indigenous bird life to provide the protein they needed. The moa was the most obvious source of flesh (apart from other Maori, cannibalism being an accepted reward of victory in battle), but once the larger, more obvious birds had been captured, the hunters sought the flightless kiwi, the weka, and the kaka. The

Black birch forest lining a West Coast road in the 1880s. The forests of New Zealand have suffered since the arrival of both the Maori and the European. The burning of dense forest, too difficult to clear manually, led to a wholesale destruction of the bush that was to have serious repercussions in later years. By 1868, a quarter of the North Island forests had been destroyed, and by the turn of the century New Zealand was a tamed land. However, due to a greater awareness of the country's natural heritage much of the remaining bush is now protected in national parks.

South Island goose disappeared sometime between the fourteenth and sixteenth centuries, the large New Zealand harrier about the same time, as did the *Pachyornis elephantopus,* the elephant-footed lesser moa. The Maori fowler had gradually developed his skills from catching the slow-moving moa to being able to spear or snare those species which could take to the air. Those birds which were able to retreat to the mountain fastnesses and the most impenetrable of the forests were able to survive, although in greatly reduced numbers.

For the European, the barriers were, primarily, twofold: the bush, and the hilly terrain. The first was an impediment to cultivation of the land on any large scale, the second made communications difficult and hazardous in the early years, so much so that until at least the turn of the century and the development of adequate railways, the easiest way to get from one part of the country to another was by ship.

It has been estimated that when the white man arrived in New Zealand, two-thirds of the North Island was covered in subtropical rain forest; by 1840, the European and Maori use of fire had already made inroads into the bush.

Because the bush of the North Island was so difficult to convert into pasture (not to mention the resistance of the Maori tribes, which will be covered later), the most rapid pastoral development took place in the South Island, particularly on the lush Canterbury Plains. The farmers needed space because, apart from some crops needed locally, the only viable large-scale farming was sheep, for the wool; until refrigeration, meat was a secondary consideration. The nearest potential market for meat – Australia – had plenty of its own, which it could not export either.

By 1855 the Canterbury Plains had been completely taken over by the pastoralists, many of them having come from Australia, while the English immigrants tended to keep close to Christchurch. The plains were not then the highly cultured landscape they are today, with their neat paddocks, varied coloured squares of crops and grass, tidy houses and smooth bitumen roads, lines of trees for wind-breaks and irrigation. Then it was just a seemingly unlimited sea of brown tussock, with only the mountains to the west providing any visible landmark. Beyond the plains is the high country; the term "high country" is probably more evocative for the New Zealander than any other geographical location. It is in the high country that the settler pits himself against the natural elements – the wind, rain and snow – to let his sheep and cattle roam without fences for the year and then bring them down by the means of the muster, when the men ride out into the hills for days to bring back animals which have wandered to every corner of the property. The symbol of the New Zealand way of life is the shepherd with his horse and dog, silhouetted against the peaks of the Southern Alps.

The easier country of the South Island was soon locked up by the runholders – the squatters, as they were then – and the New Zealand frontier turned back to the fringes of the North Island

43

bush. By 1881, it is estimated that only 800,000 hectares of the North Island was sown in grass. In the first years of settlement the pioneers had made their first impact on the areas closest to the coast, but between 1853 and 1881 – largely because of the Maori Wars – little real advance was made into the bush. The least troubled regions of Poverty Bay, Auckland, Wairarapa, Hawke's Bay and the Horowhenua had been penetrated, but the central part of the North Island was still largely untouched. In 1881, half the North Island contained only one per cent of New Zealand's European population. The hot lake region, the heavily forested and rugged hill country around the Rangitikei, Wanganui and Mokau rivers were, by and large, beyond the boundaries of European settlement. Fire was the answer to the heavy bush. For month after month, a great haze of smoke lay over the North Island. Edwin Stanley Brookes, in his account of frontier life in Taranaki, wrote that the burning off took place between the end of January and late March, with each clearing burning out in between a week or fourteen days, leaving charred trunks or logs to again be fired when they were properly dry. The lighter branches which survived the first blaze would be chopped into smaller pieces, then burnt. "Those who have never witnessed one of these large bush fires would scarcely believe the grand effect that is produced by them", wrote Brookes. "The vast volume of black smoke that arises after the fire brand has been applied causes a dark shadow to fall on all surrounding objects; this is accompanied by a roaring noise when, after a few seconds, flames of fire burst out to a tremendous height, disclosing a bright red furnace beneath that makes you run away from the scorching heat."

Another early account records that, in 1859, Auckland was covered by smoke for two weeks. The wholesale destruction of the bush was to have disastrous effects on the supply of timber in New Zealand in later years, and was one of the factors which brought about the massive planting of exotic forests in the 1920s. In the 1880s, for example, the entire 7000 hectare Puhipuhu kauri forest was destroyed by fire. By 1868, a quarter of the North Island forests had been destroyed. Naturally, the pioneer farmer of New Zealand did not see his workmanship as anything other than progress. Many of the North Island settlers had come to New Zealand to obtain the land they could never hope to have in Britain; it is quite clear in the quotation above that Edwin Stanley Brookes considered the great burn-offs as a wondrous sight to behold. Another early settler spoke of the "ecstacies of improvement". Another wrote: "I admit that logs and stumps are unsightly, but what of that, if you and your stock are in plenty. Every year as they dry and decay you can put a little fire into them and they will soon disappear." The settlers had a great sense of achievement in draining the swamps, fencing, growing crops and increasing their stock. They were, in their eyes, taming a wilderness, and – in the narrowest terms – the transformation of the New Zealand landscape in such a brief period was an amazing achievement.

The land was still being devastated during the first decades of the twentieth century. This photograph shows the result of a bush burn in 1907. (McAllister Collection, Alexander Turnbull Library, Wellington.)

If the fires did not kill the bird life, however, man had plenty of other tricks up his sleeve. The European introduced species from his own native land. Some were accidental – the rat and mouse – and others were intentional, intended to reproduce the sounds of the birds of Britain or to provide sport. Rats and mice took over the land quickly, but so did the bigger creatures. Pigs, with their powerful snouts, found ground-dwelling birds such as the kiwi or kakapo easy picking. Cats, which were let run wild in their thousands – on various offshore islands as well as the mainland – could catch just about any native bird; the birds had never had natural enemies like this, and were easy prey. The cats ate and decimated the native quail, kakapo, saddleback, wrens, New Zealand thrush – and many others. The cats were backed up in this reign of feral terror by introduced ferrets, stoats and weasels. The introduced goats and deer ate the bark and leaves of the trees, growing into herds of hundreds, and depriving the soil of its traditional cover. The depredations of the rabbit, not to mention the opposum and hare, are well documented and were perhaps the greatest of the several ecological disasters man has wreaked in New Zealand.

The beautiful huia, which once inhabited the great North Island forests, was last seen in 1907, but the delightful South Island kea survived man's attempt to wipe out the species. It is a notoriously inquisitive bird, attracted particularly by bright and shiny objects. Tourists in the Southern Alps today find that when they stop to take a photograph that the kea can be induced to walk to within a foot or two of the camera by dangling a tin or other shiny object. It was this inquisitiveness which led to the problem, as farmers last century became convinced that the kea was a killer of sheep. The evidence was flimsy at best, but on the basis of it the New Zealand Government offered a bounty on the bird. By 1929, the 5s bounty had been claimed on 29,000 beaks. Fortunately, the evidence is beginning to move back to the kea's favour, and it seems likely that there will be plenty of these native parrots left to steal the boots, socks and other possessions of trampers and mountaineers in the future.

Sometimes, the forest and the land exacted its price from the new settlers. Bush fires got out of control and trapped the men who had lit them; in 1888 the southern Hawke's Bay township of Norsewood (founded by Scandanavian settlers) was almost wiped out by a great fire. Falling trees crushed the pioneers, the rivers and streams swollen by sudden rainfall drowned them, and the vastness of the bush often caused many to be lost and starved to death.

By 1900, though, New Zealand was a land tamed. Certainly there were still substantial areas of bush, but the patterns of development were well established. Vast tracts of the North Island had been turned into pasture for cattle and sheep. In Taranaki by 1910 all the lowland bush had been cleared and the province was one of the richest dairying areas of New Zealand.

The improvement of communications had made much of this

development possible. Before the days when man was accustomed to air travel, the imposing landscape of New Zealand required the settlers to engineer complex methods of linking one region with another. There were a few low-lying areas, such as Canterbury or the undulating fields of Southland, but for most of the country there was always a hill, a mountain range or river in the way. Even by the 1860s there were few roads in New Zealand except those picked out by enterprising settlers or the bullock teamsters. The large rivers were spanned by ferry punts upon which the teams of twenty to thirty bullocks and their dray with its towering load of wool would be pulled across the water by rope and windlass. The smaller rivers and streams, with their shifting and perilous fords, were the much greater source of anxiety for the teamster. Even in the 1860s, however, the bullock teams operated over a relatively small area; the hauls over long distances were by pack horses, which were lucky to average three kilometres a day over hilly bush country.

New Zealand was finally colonised by the railway; more so than any of the nations of the new world, railways made possible the development of a national economy, and one whereby the movement of goods and people overland was made possible. The story of the railway system, sadly today being run down in the belief that large road lorries are most efficient in long-distance cartage, is one of skill, enterprise, foresight and – most of all – imagination and courage. At its zenith, just after World War II, the New Zealand railway system required 2600 bridges and more than 170 tunnels. In terms of the length, the wide scree rivers of the Canterbury Plains have the most notable bridges: the one across the Rakaia is 1740 metres long, the Waitaki River bridge 912 metres. Of the viaducts, most are on the North Island Main Trunk. There was a popular myth some years ago that the reason the passenger trains between Auckland and Wellington travelled overnight was that the viaducts were so high, and the track so winding, that it was best that most passengers could not see out the window. The Makatote viaduct, seventy-eight metres high and 260 metres long, was fabricated on the spot because complete girders could not be brought in on the narrow track which was the only form of transport route to the location. The nearby Hapuawhenua viaduct, forty-five metres high and 283 metres long, was one of the last great structures which were necessary before New Zealand's two major cities were linked by the steel permanent way. It was completed in 1908, just a few months before the first through train was able to travel between the country's two major cities. To build the viaduct, the workers first had to construct a tramway through the bush so that they could transport all the construction material; then incline tramways had to be built down to each pier so that the teams of workmen could take the steel and concrete down to the bottom of the valley. Even more complex arrangements had been made earlier at the Makatote site: a huge workshop was built, a quarry developed to produce stone for the works and a tramline to carry the boulders to a crusher. Power was supplied by a huge

The Otira Range, Canterbury, as shown in this 1870 etching from a drawing by Nicholas Chevalier, lies in some of New Zealand's most breath-taking country. The desire to open up a path through the mountains to the goldfields in the 1860s, a time when New Zealand had few roads, led to the building of a bridle path that soon expanded to take coaches. Work on the road was carried out in the harshest of conditions, and engineers had to battle in snow, sleet and frost against ravines, torrents, cliffs and dense forests.

portable steam engine and a dynamo – like everything else on the site, these had to be dragged through the bush by teams of bullocks. Twelve hundred tonnes of cement and more than a 1000 tonnes of steel were transported by wagon behind either horses or bullocks.

The scope of the achievement in building the Main Trunk railway is indicated by the fact that forty-four years elapsed between the first rails being laid at Auckland and the first scheduled express service. The easier land was covered by 1880 – at Te Awamutu in the north, and Marton in 1878. Ahead lay the really difficult country, the great rivers and gorges, and what is now the Tongariro National Park. There were many engineering problems, including how to get the line from the Waimarino Plateau to the Wanganui River valley, which involved a descent of 550 metres in a distance of twenty-five kilometres, with the final drop of 200 metres in just six kilometres. The surveyors had to fight their way through dense bush and over hills which had never been mapped before. The solution was to become a work of engineering genius. The man behind it was R. W. Holmes, senior engineer of the Public Works Department. He developed the notion of a spiral which would cram seven kilometres of line into a distance (by a straight line) of one and a half kilometres, allowing a descent in that distance of 130 metres. This was the famed Raurimu Spiral, and Holmes' plan was to build a complete circle (with the line running through a tunnel beneath itself), with three horseshoe curves and another tunnel. No engineer to this day has been able to come up with a better scheme for taking the line through this difficult piece of country.

Although the North Island Main Trunk was a spectacular triumph, it was not the only item of inspired engineering. Between Wellington and the Wairarapa stood the Rimutaka Ranges. The problem was that the climb was too steep for any conventional locomotive, so the engineers adopted the Fell engine, which as well as having the normal driving wheels on the two rails, also had wheels which gripped a centre rail. These locomotives were spaced throughout each train for the climb – sometimes five of them – while the descent was managed with similarly spaced brake wagons equipped with powerful hand-operated brakes which gripped the central rail. It was a costly and time-consuming operation, as each train had to be split up and re-marshalled at both top and bottom of the incline, while the brake vans had to be hauled back to the summit after each use. The incline was abandoned after completion of a tunnel through the Rimutaka Ranges in 1954, the tunnel being nine kilometres long.

This tunnel was one of many major drilling efforts made necessary by the steep high country that dominates so much of New Zealand. Before its construction, the longest tunnel was the Otira, nearly nine kilometres long, and which passed through the Southern Alps. The tracks had climbed the foothills of the Alps, and then stopped. It was not until 1907 that it was decided that some reliable link between Canterbury and the West Coast had to

The building of the Rimutaka incline in the Rimutaka Ranges was hailed in the 1880s as New Zealand's greatest engineering feat. However, the incline, which overcame climbs too steep for conventional trains, proved a costly and time-consuming operation and was abandoned in 1954 when a tunnel through the Ranges was completed.

Page 49
Tree-fern-lined stream, South Westland.
Westland's fierce little streams rush down from mountain heights
to the sea against a backdrop of dark forest and giant tree-ferns.

Pages 50/51
Kaukatea Valley, east of Wanganui.
Kaukatea Valley, near Wanganui. This land was settled early in
New Zealand's European period. The New Zealand Company
purchased much of the land from local tribes and the soil was
found to be rich and fertile.

Page 52
Tukituki Valley, Hawke's Bay.

Page 53, above
Canterbury Plains, pattern of fields.
The mosaic-like pattern of fields on the Canterbury Plains
reflects the carving up of squatters' land during the 1880s.
Shelter-belts protect the mixed crops from the dry nor'-wester.

Page 53, below
Virginian deer fawn.
Deer were introduced into New Zealand to afford the new settler
the sport he took for granted back in Europe. But introduced
animals competed with the native birds for food in the forests and
millions of dollars have been spent over the years in an attempt to
control deer numbers.

Page 54
Cape Kidnappers gannet colony.

Page 55, above
Gannet courtship display.
Between November and February each year the gannets breed at
this nature reserve at Cape Kidnappers in Hawke's Bay. The
colony can only be reached along a beach at low tide. The cape
was named by Captain Cook when a group of Maoris tried to
kidnap his Tahitian cabin boy.

Page 55, below
Courtship display of the royal albatross, Campbell Island.

Page 56
Sutherland Falls, Fiordland.
The Sutherland Falls in the heart of Fiordland in the South Island
is one of the highest waterfalls in the world and a feature of the
spectacular Milford Track.

be found. The workers not only had to contend with hazardous tunnelling conditions, but with more than 5000 millimetres of rain a year, not to mention snow and gales in the winter. Work had begun in 1908, but it was not until 1923 that trains began to pass through the Otira Tunnel. Because the tunnel dropped 260 metres in height above sea level between the Canterbury and the West Coast portals, steam locomotives were out of the question. They would have been greatly restricted in load to make the climb within the tunnel, and nine kilometres of running a steam locomotive, and one working hard on the gradient, would have been impossible for the engine's crew and distinctly unpleasant for passengers. So it was that the Otira, then the longest tunnel in what was the British Empire, became New Zealand's first electrified railway.

The struggle against the natural barriers continues to this day. In September 1978 the completion of the most recent tunnel through the Kaimai Ranges provided a new direct railway line to the Bay of Plenty. This tunnel is now the longest in New Zealand, thirteen metres longer than the Rimutaka tunnel. Between the Waikato and Bay of Plenty, the Kaimai Ranges rise to heights of 800 metres. When railways were first laid, the Ranges were too great a challenge, so the lines skirted around the edges, making for time-consuming and circuitous routes. The new line had been justified by the huge growth of traffic from the exotic forests of the North Island. The large mill at Kinleith and a redeveloped port at Mt Manganui had to be linked.

It was these forests which represent another significant transformation of the New Zealand landscape. In pre-*pakeha* times, the interior of the North Island south of the Hot Lakes district had been an island within the huge forests. This region was typified by volcanic ash, tutu and tussock. In the early years of the century, it was found that this region could support exotic trees, particularly *Pinus radiata,* a native of North America. By the 1920s, timber was in short supply. The great native forests had produced fine timbers (the Royal Navy sought kauri for ships' spars, the Maoris made their canoes from trunks of totara, and more recently since European settlement there had grown to be a substantial market for wood in Australia) but the wholesale burnings had wiped out much of the nation's timber resources. By 1922, only 19,000 hectares of exotic timber had been planted, but then followed a boom in Government-funded planting, with 20,000 hectares being planted in one year alone.

A Royal Commission in 1913 had come to the conclusion that native trees simply did not grow fast enough if the forests were to be replaced. Native trees took between two and three hundred years to reach full maturity; by contrast, exotic trees – radiata, larch and Douglas Fir – would mature in twenty-five years. The economics were obvious.

The result was the creation of Kiangaroa – the largest man-made forest in the world. In 1952, the timber-processing industry was growing apace as the trees matured. In 1952, £600,000 worth of exotic timber was exported, a figure doubled within four years. In 1955, New Zealand first exported paper pulp and newsprint. In 1961, the Government again set out to increase the planting of trees in an attempt to double the area of exotic forest by the year 2000. In some years since then, State and private planting has reached 50,000 hectares.

If the record with the forests and wildlife is less than admirable, some amends have been made. New Zealand has a system of national parks which run the gamut of topography, fauna and flora, and cover more than 2 million hectares or one-thirteenth of the country's total land area. Three of the parks are in the North Island. The Urewera National Park includes lakes Waikareiti and Waikaremoana and contains major stands of native forest. It was one of the Maori strongholds during the wars of last century. Egmont National Park preserves a circle of land around the mountain, while Tongariro National Park includes the three volcanoes and part of the "Desert".

Abel Tasman National Park, one of the many reminders of the first European to discover New Zealand, lies along the coast from Nelson on Tasman Bay. It is unlike the other parks in that one of its attractions is the many clean and beautiful beaches, while further south the Nelson Lakes National Park is based on lakes Rotoroa and Rotoiti, surrounded by mountains including Mt Travers (2331 metres). The Arthur's Pass National Park, through which passes the tortuous road which is the shortest route between Christchurch and Greymouth, incorporates the range of grandeur one would expect in the Southern Alps – towering mountains, deep valleys, waterfalls and rushing rivers. The Alps are included in three other National Parks – Mt Cook, Westland and Mt Aspiring, while the southernmost, Fiordland National Park, is at 1.2 million hectares one of the largest national parks in the world.

Fiordland is the home of two great lakes mentioned in the first chapter, Te Anav and Manapouri. Through it also runs one of the great motoring adventures, the Milford Road. This road is frequently under threat of avalanche and has the eerie Homer Tunnel. This tunnel was carved through solid rock, and some of the workmen involved in the project were killed by avalanches. Work began on it in 1935, but it was not until 1954 that it was opened to private cars. It was completed by men who toiled in conditions at least equal to those which prevailed at the Otira Tunnel. Fiordland is the wildest region of New Zealand, now largely unpopulated but once the witness to the whalers and sealers who preceded the colonising settlers. There was also gold and timber which gave rise to two overnight towns in the far south, Te Oneroa and Cromarty. The latter had hotels, general stores and boarding houses; in 1892, they even held a regatta there. Today nothing remains except for a few fragments of buildings and debris of long-ago human occupation.

Apart from national parks, New Zealand has more than a thousand scenic reserves which preserve areas of scenic interest (the Wanganui River in the North Island, the Buller Gorge in the

The nikau palm, the southernmost palm of all, grows in lowland forests of the North Island, and appears as far south as Banks Peninsula and Hokitika in the South Island, and in the Chatham Islands. The single-stemmed plant grows up to thirty feet in height and bears large fronds that measure between four and eight feet long. The nikau palm has large flowers and small, red, fleshy fruit with a kernel. The Maori used the nikau leaves to make woven articles, while the top of the stem, which is fleshy and juicy, is sometimes eaten.

South, for example), with historic reserves declared for a range of sites from landing places of Tasman and Cook to locations of battles during the Maori Wars. Nature reserves, of which there are fifty, provide protection for flora and fauna; they include the Cape Kidnappers gannet colony, the white heron colony in Westland, and the albatross colony at the mouth of Otago Harbour. All the sub-Antarctic islands are classified as nature reserves.

The Wildlife Service of the Department of Internal Affairs is an agency dedicated to saving what is left of New Zealand's bird life. All but three common species of native bird are protected by legislation, and the highest priority is given to those birds which are vulnerable or in danger of extinction.

One of the few good pieces of news was the discovery in 1948 that the takahe, or notornis as it is more popularly known, which was thought to be extinct was still alive in the remote Takahe Valley in Fiordland National Park. Since then a mammoth effort has been made to increase the numbers of the bird, now estimated to be between 200 and 250 in the wild. It was found that the main reason for the bird's decline as late as the 1960s was competition for food with the introduced red deer. Since then the Forest Service stepped up deer shooting and the alpine grasslands have improved. The Wildlife Service has tried to protect the takahe in the wild, but the breeding rate is low with only about 40 per cent of chicks surviving the first three months. Since 1976 several takahe have been hatched at the Mt Bruce Native Bird Reserve with the intention that when there were sufficient numbers of birds bred in captivity, they would be transferred to Maud Island in the Marlborough Sounds which has been designated as a sanctuary for endangered birds.

The real hope for the endangered species is the protection of a number of offshore islands where rats, cats and humans can be controlled or prevented from landing. The Chatham Islands robin, probably the most endangered bird species in the world, was down to nine birds in 1980, all of them on Little Mangere Island. By 1976 the total population was seven, and they were then transferred to Mangere Island where the Wildlife Service had previously planted thousands of suitable native trees and shrubs and had removed the sheep. Since the move, the birds have reproduced and revived some hope for their survival.

The threat, even on the islands, is ever-present: in 1962, rats were introduced (probably by means of fishing boats) to Big South Cape Island and two other islands off the southern tip of Stewart Island. Until then, the population of the South Island saddleback was several thousand. The rats quickly began to exterminate the saddleback, and the Wildlife Service mounted a rescue operation, transferring those surviving birds which could be found to other islands which the rat had not reached. The South Island species is now thought to number about three hundred.

While the brown teal, the rarest of New Zealand's native waterfowl, was in no immediate danger of extinction, the Service began in the 1960s to plan how it could prevent that danger ever

Lake Tekapo, the bed of an ancient glacier in the central South Island, is one of many lakes throughout the Southern Alps whose serenity combines with the majesty of the surrounding mountains to create a scene of world standing.

arising. Birds were taken to the Mt Bruce Reserve and the teal proved to be a breeder in captivity, and by 1979 more than 140 had been liberated in areas where they had once been common, in an attempt to re-establish a population there. By 1979, it was accepted that the bird would breed after release with the sighting of a pair with a duckling at one of the liberation areas at Pukepuke Lagoon.

For the Forbes' parakeet, the threat was from the Chatham Islands red-crowned parakeet and a hybrid strain which adapted well to the changing vegetation on Mangere Island and began to displace the Forbes' parakeet. The solution was to remove the competing birds from the two islands, and as a result the Forbes' parakeet doubled its numbers.

It is an uphill battle, and of all the endangered bird species listed by the International Union for Conservation of Nature and Natural Resources, about 11 per cent are from New Zealand or its outlying islands.

3. Outlying Islands

Out in the vast oceans which surround New Zealand are several small dots on the map. These outlying islands range from the subtropical Kermadec group to the north, the temperate Chathams to the east, and the sub-Antarctic groups which consist of The Snares, Bounty Island, Antipodes Island, the Auckland Islands and Campbell Island. All the islands have a brief, but rich, history of human contact. But it is the sub-Antarctic islands which are of the greatest present interest due to their variety of birds and mammals, and they are all now designated as reserves to afford full protection. The importance of these islands is considerable in the scientific world: not only are some of the islands relatively untouched by man – there are ecosystems not found elsewhere in the world – but many of the species would face the danger of extinction if these refuges did not exist. The damage caused by sealing parties may never be repaired, but at least now sea-lions and seals are once again to be found in considerable numbers in the region; the giant southern royal albatross flies unmolested over the oceans, and several species of penguin breed each year in peace.

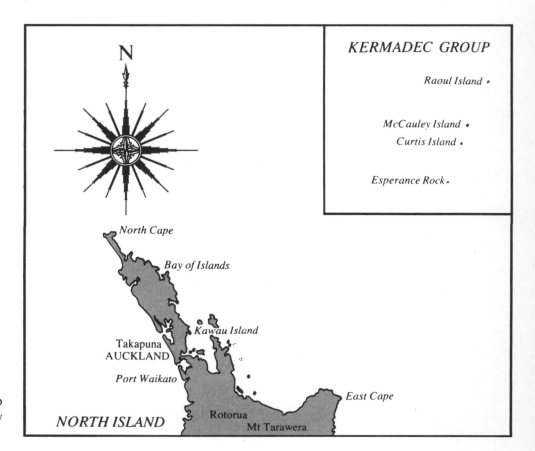

Map showing the location of the Kermadec group of islands, to the north of the North Island of New Zealand.

61

Of all the islands, only the Chathams remain populated (with the exception of meteorological bases at the Kermadecs and Campbell). The Chathams cover 963 square kilometres and have a population of less than 600 people. It was once the home for the Moriori people, who were earlier settlers, it is believed, than the Maori. There were probably only about 1000 of them before European settlement, and the last Moriori died before World War II. Today the main occupations are farming and fishing, and there is an air service to the mainland 800 kilometres away. The climate, while temperate, is not always pleasant, with frequent high winds and many long periods of overcast sky, although rainfall is not notably high by New Zealand standards.

More than 900 kilometres to the north of the mainland is the Kermadec group. The main island, Raoul, has seen several attempts at settlement. Early whalers called regulary, and two families began to farm there in 1837. The farming continued for more than thirty years, but a volcanic eruption in 1872 caused the last family to leave; the group is still subjected to frequent and sometimes violent earthquakes. In 1878 the settlers came back in the form of the Bell family, who were joined briefly by others; they stayed until evacuated at the outbreak of war during 1914. The islands were used during World War I as a hiding place by the German merchant raider, *Wolf,* which preyed on the nearby shipping lanes. The Germans surprised several vessels and sank them after removing useful supplies. The *Wolf* also laid mines off the coasts of Australia and New Zealand that were considered responsible for at least two ships being sunk. During World War II a coastwatching station and radio station were maintained on Raoul Island, and after the war some farming was continued. The group is of considerable scientific importance, being the only land area in this latitude of the Pacific apart from Norfolk and Lord Howe islands, which are Australian territory, and Juan Fernandez which is Chilean. A number of Pacific sea-birds breed in large colonies on the islands of the Kermadec group, and there are a number of sub-species, such as the Kermadec storm petrel, which are endemic. Unfortunately the rats and cats brought to Raoul at various times have ruthlessly reduced bird life. The Kermadec petrel, which once numbered tens of thousands on Raoul, was reduced to a handful of birds; luckily the other islands of the group were not affected.

The most northerly of the islands which lie between New Zealand and the Antarctic are The Snares, the largest of the group being only 260 hectares in area. There is no harbour for large ships, and there are a number of rock stacks and a chain of islets. Several creeks on the main island flow all year, but the water is putrid from the droppings of the thousands of birds on the island so that any human parties have to land their own water supplies. The number of birds on the island has never been conclusively counted, but one respectable estimate several years ago placed the population at about 5 million. The sooty shearwater is the most numerous at between two and three million birds. There are three

Whaling commenced in New Zealand waters only twenty-two years after Captain James Cook's first voyage to the country. The industry boomed in 1839 when sixty-two American whaling ships were recorded as having entered the Bay of Islands. Whaling ships called at the settlement on Raoul Island in the Kermadec group, while an unsuccessful attempt to establish a whaling industry at the Auckland Islands was launched in 1849.

land birds unique to the islands: the Snares Islands snipe, the fernbird and the tomtit. The endemic Snares Islands penguin festoons the slopes and valleys with its colonies during the breeding season. The beautiful Buller's mollymawk is unique to New Zealand, breeding only at The Snares, on the Chatham Islands and on Solander Island.

The Snares were ravaged by sealing gangs and although one group of four men was stranded there between 1810 and 1817, the islands have rarely been visited in the last century and a half. A castaways' depot was maintained by the New Zealand Government until 1928 in case of shipwreck. A scientific party which visited the main island in the summer of 1946–1947 described it as a "magnificent place, outstanding because it is perhaps the only one of any size now left in New Zealand which still retains its virgin state". Miraculously, none of the destructive cats or rats, or any other predatory mammal, has become established on The Snares.

The largest, and best known, of the sub-Antarctic islands are the Aucklands. Over 600 square kilometres in area, this group has the most varied landscape and flora of all the islands, including some magnificent rata forest. The islands were colonised in 1849 by the Southern Whale Fishery Company which landed white settlers to join a small community of Maori, the idea being that the colony at Port Ross would raise food for itself and service the ships sailing the roaring forties from Australia to Cape Horn. It was a failure from the start. The white settlers were horrified to find a land that was peat swamp and tangled scrub. It was difficult to walk any distance, let alone cultivate. Screaming winds and pouring rain, even in the middle of summer, completed the welcome. Anyway, despite initial hardship they started building a settlement. Added to the physical trials were those imposed by Lieutenant-Governor Enderby, high-handed in the extreme, who was described as both chief lawmaker and law-breaker. The settlers got along reasonably well with the Maori people on the island, although there were outbreaks of trouble when sailors gave the native people liquor or tried to take their women.

While some ships called, the attempts to catch whales were not very successful, so that the sperm oil which had been intended to provide a good income for the settlers was not forthcoming. The New Zealand Governor, Sir George Grey, visited the settlement in late 1850 and came away as pessimistic about its future as the settlers had already become. The next year two special commissioners forcibly removed Enderby from the Auckland Islands after he refused to resign; the colony had cost the company £30,000, had produced revenue of less than a tenth of that, and was generally in a hopeless state. It was soon decided to abandon the islands.

The only attention given the group for many decades was when news of several shipwrecks filtered through to the mainland. The most spectacular of these occurred in 1866 when the *General Grant*, carrying passengers and gold from Australia, was wrecked, leading the Southland Provincial Council to establish castaways'

Sir George Grey, New Zealand Governor 1845–1853, visited the cold and windswept settlement at the Aucklands late in 1850. Not then a decade old, the group of islands was struggling to support the whaling industry established when the islands were colonised by the Southern Whale Fishery Company in 1849. Sir George left the islands feeling pessimistic about their future; not long afterwards they were abandoned.

Page 65
Rugged coastline, Antipodes Island.
Antipodes Island, one of the most remote islands in the southern ocean, remains uninhabited and is still largely in its natural state.

Pages 66/67
Adams Island and Carnley Harbour from Mount Dick, the Aucklands.
Adams Island, showing the western part of Carnley Harbour from Mount Dick, is in the Auckland group. Attempts to establish a whaling station and sheep and cattle grazing on the windswept and cold Aucklands were abandoned long ago. Descendants of the cattle left to roam on Enderby, the northernmost island, were discovered in 1973 by a scientific party.

Page 68, above
Birdlife on Campbell Island.
Grey-headed mollyhawks and black-browed albatross can be found on Campbell Island, the most southern of the New Zealand territories. The island is fascinating to scientists as a habitat for feral sheep (abandoned after several attempts to establish a wool-producing venture) which have formed social patterns unknown in domesticated sheep.

Page 68, middle
The grey-coloured, light-mantled sooty albatross.
The exquisite grey-coloured, light-mantled sooty albatross, with its semi-circle of white feathers behind the eye, is found on Campbell Island.

Page 68, below
Hooker's sea-lion, The Snares.
Hooker's sea-lions, found on The Snares, the Aucklands and Campbell Island, are aggressive towards man. The sea-lion population was decimated by sealing parties in the early nineteenth century.

Page 69
Fernbird, The Snares.
A fernbird at The Snares, a superbly scenic and unspoiled group of islands.

Page 70
Erect-crested penguins, Antipodes Island.
Erect-crested penguins on a rocky shore of Antipodes Island.

Page 71
Colony of crested penguins and chicks, The Snares.
A crowded colony of crested penguins live with their chicks in a communal creche on The Snares.

Page 72
Bleak Ewing Island.
Ewing Island is part of the Auckland Islands, a place of peat swamp and tangled scrub, screaming winds and pouring rain.

Page 73, above
Bulbinella meadow, Enderby Island.
A meadow of the colourful bulbinella plant on Enderby Island in the Aucklands.

Page 73, below
Monument Harbour and La Botte Rock, Campbell Island.
Campbell Island, of all New Zealand's outlying territories, is the most changed by man, being farmed between 1895 and 1931. Pictured here is Monument Harbour, and La Botte Rock that lies just off the island's coast.

Page 74
Moorland, Enderby Island.
The landscape and flora of the Aucklands group is the most varied of all the islands. This bleak moorland is on Enderby Island.

Page 75
Grasslands, Auckland Island.
Rolling, tussock grasslands are a feature in the high tops above Musgrave Inlet on the largest island in the Aucklands group. The serenity of the scene belies the ferocity of the southern ocean that caused disastrous shipwrecks in the days when sailing vessels plied the roaring forties.

Page 76
Wildflowers, Campbell Island.
Wildflowers dot the grasslands that sweep up to St Col Ridge on Campbell Island.

depots with food and clothing on the islands, the remains of which are still quite evident today. One of the most amazing tales is that of the crew of the small schooner *Grafton* which was wrecked at the islands at the beginning of 1864, the survivors living on seal meat and whatever else they could forage. In July 1865, facing the reality that they would not be rescued, three of the men set off in a maskeshift boat with sails for New Zealand, being almost sunk by mountainous seas, but reaching Stewart Island on the fifth day. They had to be lifted from their boat as they were too weak to stand.

In the 1890s, an Invercargill farmer obtained a pastoral lease and attempted to graze sheep and cattle on the Aucklands, but it became too expensive to hire ships to transport stock. In 1973, a scientific party counted thirty-nine descendants of the original cattle roaming wild on Enderby, the northernmost island in the group. Forty-nine bird species breed in the Auckland Islands, while the long white beach on Enderby Island is crowded with sea-lions in the summer.

The most remote of the outlying islands are Bounty and Antipodes. Little has been known about the Antipodes until recent times. It was the home of a large colony of fur seals, but these were wiped out in 1804 when an American gang was marooned there for two years and returned to Sydney with 60,000 skins. For the next fifty years nothing was heard of Antipodes Island. In 1893, the ship *Spirit of Dawn* was wrecked there, the crew sheltering in a cave for eighty-seven days, the weather being so appalling they could not explore the island. Few ships call there today as there is no safe anchorage, but in 1975 two young Englishmen visited Antipodes Island, it being the goal of a wager that they could not reach the islands travelling from London on their own resources. The stayed an hour. Antipodes Island is still largely in its natural state and penguins, albatross and at least ten species of petrel breed there.

Nearly 800 kilometres to the east of New Zealand lie the Bounty Islands, a group of granite rocks totalling two square kilometres of land area. They were discovered by Captain William Bligh in 1788, and named after the ship later to become involved in the famous mutiny. There is no vegetation, nor permanent streams, and the sealing gangs marooned there must have suffered frightful conditions. The rock surface of the islands is almost totally covered with sea-birds, with penguins numbering in the millions in the summer months, and joined by large concentrations of a few other species.

Campbell Island is the most southerly of the New Zealand territories and of all the islands, is the most changed by man, being farmed between 1895 and 1931. During World War II coastwatching parties were established there; these were superseded after the war by a meteorological post.

Campbell was discovered in 1810 and named after the ship's owners, Campbell and Company of Sydney. As on the other islands, the seals were quickly reduced to tiny numbers. But the story of the sheep is an extraordinary one. The first flocks were taken to the island in 1895, when the Government granted a grazing lease. For fifty years, one pastoralist after another tried to make a success of the enterprise. One of the leaseholders brought in shepherds from the Shetland Islands but they fared little better than others before or after. At the height of the farming 8000 sheep were being shorn but the dreadful weather and the distance from the market proved too much. It rains on Campbell for all but thirty days of the year. Gales blow most of the time and the seas between the island and the mainland are usually treacherous.

The Great Depression of 1929 was the final blow. The wool was worth so little by 1930 that the leaseholder's agent decided that the charter of a ship that year could not be financially justified. It took more than twelve months for public pressure to force the Government to rescue the men. They were found in tatters, living off a bleak diet of mutton and tea.

When the last shepherd left, there were 4000 sheep abandoned on the island. Some would have died off quickly, but enough adapted to the environment – and to not being shorn – for the flock to survive until the present day. Not only did the sheep adapt to shedding their wool, they now grow a third less wool than they would if they were on a mainland farm. They formed social groupings never found in mainland sheep, the females living in family groups based on the oldest ewe, while the rams graze in bachelor groups. In 1961 the sheep were estimated to number 1000, but since then the population has grown steadily. A fence was built across the island in 1970 and the sheep driven to the southern side. The result was that natural vegetation flourished since it was no longer being grazed; there was no evidence, however, that the sheep interfered with bird life on the island.

The most spectacular of the birds is the southern royal albatross, a giant bird, but tame. For nesting it seeks out the more sheltered slopes of the island where the vegetation is thicker. At the last count there were nearly 5000 breeding pairs on Campbell. Other birds include various species of penguin, grey-headed mollymawks, skuas and the beautiful grey-coloured light-mantled sooty albatross. Unfortunately, cats and rats have taken great toll of the petrel population. While the birds thrive on the slopes, the sea-lions and seals are now more numerous on the beaches during summer, while elephant seals are also becoming more evident.

All the sub-Antarctic islands are designated as "Reserve for the Preservation of Flora and Fauna" and permits to land there are required from the Department of Lands and Survey, which administers the islands. These areas are of immense value both in scientific terms and as a safe habitat for many species in a world where safe habitats are few in number. They are of world importance.

4. People of New Zealand

New Zealand is a land of immigrants. All its people have come from across the sea, from the original Polynesians, to the great waves of European migration after 1840, to the more recent post-war groups such as the Dutch and Pacific Islanders. The patterns of population continue to change; for example, in the years between 1961 and 1976, the Maori population jumped from 167,086 to 270,035, which reflects the staggering resurgence of the Maori people. The huge growth in Maori population plus the migration from the Cook Islands, Nuie and Samoa, have altered the racial equation in New Zealand, especially in a city such as Auckland which is truly the capital of Polynesia.

The majority of European New Zealanders are descended from English stock, so that it is not surprising that nearly a million of them give their religious denomination as Church of England. Practically all the first settlements from 1840 were initiated in England. Wellington and Nelson were settled from the southern counties, Taranaki from Cornwall and Devon. The Church of England was behind the colonisation of Christchurch and the Canterbury Province. It was intended by the Anglicans to faithfully replicate the idealised notion of English society. Migrants would have to be members of the Church of England, of good character, so that a proper moral atmosphere was created from the outset. This miniature England was to accommodate the full range of people, from the Bishop at its head to the skilled artisan

Christchurch in 1852. This sketch shows Christchurch, now the largest city in the South Island and the commercial centre of the rich Canterbury Plains, in 1852, not long after it was colonised by the Church of England. Modelled upon the English cathedral town of the same name, Christchurch retains her own cathedral and square as the heart of the city. Situated on the Avon and Heathcote rivers, this beautiful city, known as the 'Garden City' due to the foresight of early developers, who set aside the 1500-acre Hagley Park, retains the English charm and atmosphere bestowed upon it by her founders.

and labourer at the bottom. The city of Christchurch was modelled on the English cathedral town, with the roading system radiating outwards from the cathedral at its centre.

The Scots were scarce among the first shiploads of migrants to New Zealand. All that changed in 1848 when the ships carrying settlers despatched by the Otago Association arrived at Dunedin. The association had first called itself the Lay Association of the Free Church of Scotland, and two-thirds of the early settlers professed allegiance to the Presbyterian Church. Dunedin is itself the ancient name for Edinburgh, and its main streets are Princes and George, just as in Edinburgh. It has retained its character: the Presbyterian Church dominates the religious life of the city; the two major private schools are Presbyterian. The Scots also settled in large numbers in the southernmost city of Invercargill, named after Captain William Cargill, one of the chief promoters of the Otago Association. Dunedin, as a footnote, has the only kilt shop in New Zealand.

The other European races never settled in any substantial numbers. Those who did were quickly absorbed by the forces of homogeneity, and New Zealand never experienced the urban racial concentrations which could be clearly identified in turn-of-the-century New York, or even present day Sydney and Melbourne. Fifty-seven French settlers arrived at Akaroa in Canterbury, but their only lasting mark was to bequeath French names to the area. A few attempts were made by German groups to bring their nationals to New Zealand; some settled near Nelson while a group of German-speaking Bohemians founded a settlement at Puhoi, north of Auckland. The Scandinavians settled the area in southern Hawke's Bay (one of the towns there is called Norsewood) and northern Wairarapa; most were Danes, but there were many also from Sweden and Norway.

Of the more recent waves of European migrants, the policy of New Zealand governments has been to encourage settlers either from the British Isles or from northern Europe. The need for migrants to quickly assimilate and adopt the New Zealand way of life has been uppermost. While the British continued to dominate post-war migration, one other group stood out: the Dutch. The need to find a new home after the Netherlands East Indies became independent Indonesia, and the difficult post-war conditions in Holland, were incentives for many Dutch to migrate to New Zealand. Between 1950 and 1963, 25,000 moved to New Zealand and they left a marked impression on the New Zealanders at the time. The Dutch were remarkable not only for their industry and diligence, but for their unconcealed enthusiasm to melt into the society by learning English quickly and intermarrying with New Zealanders.

New Zealand has always been reluctant to welcome Asian peoples, but substantial numbers of Chinese and Indians did manage to establish themselves. Both racial groups have tended to maintain themselves apart from the rest of society, which may be explained by the repressive official attitude taken toward them in

The South Island city of Invercargill and the Cargill Fountain in Dunedin (shown here) pay tribute to Captain William Cargill, one of the chief promoters of the Otago Association and the first superintendent of the Otago settlement which he helped found. Situated in the square opposite the customs house, the fountain was erected by voluntary subscriptions and is one of Dunedin's landmarks.

Princes Street, Dunedin, in 1883. In the 1880s, Princes Street, Dunedin, named in honour of Edinburgh's main street, was reported to be one of the finest in the colonies, with an impressive array of buildings that purportedly were surpassed by very few in the southern hemisphere. Celebrations last century, such as the one pictured, were never without a pipe band fitted out in their appropriate tartans. The townsfolk came alive at these festivities, and often followed the pipers to large recreational areas on the edge of the town where they played Scottish games. The centre of Dunedin remained deserted until the pipes could be heard again, indicating that the holiday-makers were returning to their homes.

the past. Between 1907 and 1952, for example, no Chinese could apply to become a naturalised New Zealander. Most of the Chinese originally arrived to work on the goldfields. When the gold ran out, they entered market gardening, fruit and vegetable retailing, and the laundry and restaurant businesses. A great number of fruit and vegetable shops throughout New Zealand are still in Chinese hands. There are more than 14,000 Chinese in New Zealand today and, as a community, they are particularly noted for being the most law-abiding group of all, and the days of anti-Chinese feeling are well and truly a thing of the past. The migrants from India have not yet established a niche in New Zealand society, and have tended to remain in lower paid occupations.

The migrants from Yugoslavia are among New Zealand's most successful. The first workers settled in North Auckland where many worked digging kauri gum. Then they gradually settled the land, and became highly regarded farmers. From dairy and orchard farming, it was a short step to growing grapes, and the Yugoslav community deserves much of the credit for developing a wine industry in New Zealand. In 1979, New Zealanders consumed thirty-five times the quantity of wine that was drunk in 1940, and from a country where once wine was not a part of most people's lives, today New Zealand wines are exported as far afield as Britain.

The one controversial area of immigration policy concerns the Pacific Islanders. In recent years, measures have been taken to restrict long-term entry of Fijians and Samoans, but the people of the Cook Islands and Nuie carry New Zealand passports and have the right to settle in New Zealand. Unemployment is high in most of the Pacific nations; the people there see New Zealand as a place where they can get a job, get good health care, and education for their children. A young man or woman can earn enough in New

Zealand to support his or her family at home, and the economies of the island nations are variously dependent on money remitted home from their nationals living in New Zealand. In the years from 1966 to 1976, the Pacific Island Polynesian population in New Zealand trebled, most of the new arrivals settling in Auckland. Unfortunately, most of the Pacific Islanders are at the bottom of the socio-economic pile, with the men labouring or doing other menial work, while many of the women work in factories or in domestic duties.

Most of the Polynesian migrants have a strong attachment to their church. On Sunday morning in Auckland, the women and children dress themselves brightly to go to church, while the men don dark suits. Most of the Cook Islanders, for example, belong to the Cook Islands Christian Church which was established by the London Missionary Society.

If the church has provided a pillar for the Polynesian trying to come to terms with New Zealand life, then Maori people found support in a church as they strove to re-establish themselves after the massive dislocation caused by European domination. Many turned to the religious denominations offered by the *pakeha;* others evolved their own Maori churches, such as the Ratana Church. It was founded by Tahupotiki Wiremu Ratana, a faith healer, in 1920, at a time when the Maoris numbered just over 50,000 and were greatly demoralised. A temple was built at Ratana *pa,* near Wanganui, where today the village offers a close-knit and supportive society for its members. The church has gradually moved away from Anglican forms of worship. In the 1930s, with the rise of the Labour Party, the Ratana Church was closely identified with the Labour movement and for decades all the four Maori members of Parliament were members of the church. In 1976, more than 35,000 people gave their denomination as Ratana.

After the iniquities of the Maori Wars and the subsequent land confiscations, there has been much about *pakeha*-Maori relations to be cheerful about. Maori culture is considered by European New Zealanders as part of their own culture – the New Zealand rugby football team performs hakas, the Maori war dance, before international test matches, for example – and Maori names for places, birds and plants have been preserved. Maori art is being widely appreciated by *pakehas.*

The Maori people produced leaders of great ability at the right time. One, Sir James Carroll, became the first Maori Cabinet Minister in 1892 and became acting Prime Minister for short periods in 1909 and 1912. Sir Maui Pomare, who served as Minister of Health in 1923 and Minister of Internal Affairs in 1928, was a qualified doctor who was largely responsible for having sanitation inspectors appointed to Maori villages and for having Maori births and deaths registered. He tried to bring the Maori into the system in another way: by working to have Maori men conscripted in World War I just as the *pakeha* men already were. He also worked tirelessly to win compensation for land confisca-

Sir Maui Pomare, c. 1922–1931. The grandson of one of the few women who signed the Treaty of Waitangi, Sir Maui Pomare spent most of his life trying to improve the living standards and the status of the Maori. Having graduated in America as an M. D. in 1899, he returned to New Zealand and became a Health Officer for one of the nineteen districts created by the Maori Councils Act in 1900. Elected to the House of Representatives for Western Maori in 1911, Sir Maui served as Minister of the Cook Islands (1916), Minister of Health (1923) and Minister of Internal Affairs (1928). He was knighted in 1922 and died eight years later on a visit to Los Angeles. (Tesla Collection, Alexander Turnbull Library, Wellington.)

tion. As Minister of the Cook Islands, his efforts were directed to improving the education system there and bringing the fruit trade under Government control. Perhaps the greatest of the Maori leaders was Apirana Ngata, the first Maori to graduate from a New Zealand university. He entered Parliament in 1905 and served as Minister for Native Affairs from 1928 to 1934. He organised a scheme to bring undeveloped Maori land into production and fought for improved Maori education which he believed was the key to the raising of living standards. Ngata was greatly interested in Maori art, and encouraged the work on meeting houses and memorials to achieve the highest standards of carving. Also in the political arena was Sir Peter Buck, who graduated from Otago University in 1904 with medical degrees and served as a Maori health officer for three years. He was, briefly, Minister of the Maori Race in Massey's first cabinet of 1912, then served in the army as a medical officer at Gallipoli. But Sir Peter's major work was in the field of anthropology of Pacific Polynesian societies. His work provided a magnificent basis upon which further scientific work was done.

In giving the Maori a knowledge of their past Buck initiated an increasing awareness of Maori identity and Maoritanga. He was hopeful that eventually the two races of New Zealand would become more closely aligned. New Zealanders have gone some way towards this: intermarriage has grown steadily since the end of World War II. Now, one in eleven New Zealanders has at least half Maori ancestry, while another 86,000 New Zealanders are part, but less than half, Maori.

In 1983, the Department of Maori Affairs reported that Maori society was undergoing a major revolution, that there was a realisation that Maori people themselves had both the resources and the ability to cure many of their long-standing problems. Today, new child centres are attempting to make Maori children bilingual by the time they are five years old, the latest of several improvements aimed at rehabilitating the Maori language, the old policy of trying to assimilate the Maori totally with European culture having been abandoned. Without the Maori language, the survival of Maori culture would be impossible.

Because the white population came largely from the British Isles, and was generally from the middle and labouring classes, New Zealand developed along egalitarian lines, which in turn demanded conformity, not to be unexpected in such a small population. What New Zealand would have been like had the range of racial origins been greater, including say southern and eastern Europe, can only be a matter for speculation.

For better or worse, the average New Zealander lives in a wooden or brick detached house, with a section of land on which he or she will grow a few vegetables or flowers. They will own a car and a colour television set. Red meat, butter, milk, eggs and cheese make up a large part of the average diet. Despite the richness of such food, the average New Zealander will live until sixty-nine (if male) and seventy-six (if female). Most men will,

Sir Apirana Ngata, 1874–1950. Sir Apirana Ngata was the first Maori to graduate from a New Zealand university and was one of the first New Zealanders to hold a BA LLB. Rather than making a name for himself in law, Apirana worked with the Maori in a bid to raise their educational level and thereby, he determined, their living standards. He also stimulated a revival of interest in the language, history and tradition both of the Maoris and Polynesians. Sir Apirana was elected to Parliament in 1905, where he served under Ward and Forbes. He was knighted for his services to the Maori in 1927, and died in 1950 at the age of seventy-six. (Free Lance Collection, Alexander Turnbull Library, Wellington.)

Page 85
Kare Kare beach, mussel picking.
The mussel is a favoured food of the Maori people and they can often be seen picking them from the rocks. This rich harvest is at Kare Kare beach, west of Auckland.

Page 86, above left
Harold Jacobs, mountaineer.
Tramping and mountaineering are among the most challenging of New Zealand's many outdoor sports. Harold Jacobs is one of the present generation of mountaineers.

Page 86, above right
Rodney Dickson.
New Zealand has produced many fine runners over the years. In the tradition of Olympic medal winners Peter Snell and John Walker comes Rod Dickson whose recent achievements include winning the New York marathon. While most runners compete strictly on an amateur basis, the athletic scene is highly competitive and each day thousands of New Zealanders take to the roads and footpaths.

Page 86, below left
Sir Edmund Hillary.
One of the most famous New Zealanders, Sir Edmund Hillary was the first man to climb Mount Everest. Since then he has spent much of his energy trying to improve education and health facilities in Nepal.

Page 86, below right
Mrs Hapimana.
There are few Maoris today who wear the traditional facial tattoo.

Page 87
Tauranga waterfront.
Although it has never attracted a great number of participants, rowing has developed as one of New Zealand's more notable sports, and rowers have won Olympic medals.

Page 88
Horse-training, Woodend Beach.
Before the big race. Horses out on a training run at Woodend Beach, in North Canterbury.

Page 89
Yacht regatta, Auckland.
Closer to the city, Auckland stands astride two harbours. It is reputed to have the largest number of yachts per head of population in the world and regattas such as this are regular events.

Page 90
Horse-jumping, A. & P. Show, Christchurch.
The horse is the king of New Zealand's animals, with thoroughbred breeding an important part of the world racing scene. Here is another side of horse sport – a show-jumping event at Christchurch.

Page 91, above left
Crowds at Riccarton Cup.
New Zealand has more race-meetings than days of the year, and betting is a major source of tax revenue for the Government. Race-meetings in the main cities, such as this one at Riccarton in Christchurch, are occasions for people to display their new fashions. It is also one of the few places in New Zealand where you can still see a large number of men wearing hats, a practice otherwise largely abandoned in this country.

Page 91, above right
Maori footballers at Ngaruawahia.
Rugby permeates all parts of New Zealand society, and the Maori players have shown themselves particularly adept at the game.

Page 91, below
Lancaster Park, Canterbury v. British Lions.
The national sport is Rugby Union football, and the major competitors are Australia, South Africa, France and the four unions in Britain – England, Scotland, Wales and Ireland. When the British come to New Zealand, they usually come as a combined British Lions side and can always pack a stadium. Here at Lancaster Park in Christchurch they play the Canterbury provincial side.

Page 92
Maori woman.
A Maori wahine (woman) in traditional native dress with greenstone tiki and implement. Greenstone was a prized stone of the Maori people.

Page 93
Boating on the Avon.
Boating on the Avon River which glides peacefully through Christchurch, that most English of cities.

Page 94, above
Cricket, Boys High, Christchurch.
Boys playing cricket at Christchurch. Each Saturday morning, young New Zealanders take to the sporting grounds throughout the land. While Rugby Union and cricket dominate in their respective seasons, sizable numbers of youngsters play tennis, hockey, soccer, Rugby League and netball.

Page 94, below
Ngaruawahia Regatta Axe competition.
Husky bushmen wield their axes in competition at Ngaruawahia.

Page 95
Golf-course, St Clair, Dunedin.
While it does not get the newspaper and television exposure of other sports, golf has taken a major hold in New Zealand. Each small community has its course, and the larger cities have magnificent golf-courses, such as this one at St Clair in Dunedin.

Page 96
T & G Triangle Centre, Christchurch.
The centre of the city of Christchurch has been revitalised by imaginative planning to create civic and shopping areas in traffic-free space.

94

during their lives, play or watch rugby football and cricket. There is a good chance that he or his wife will go to the horse-races at least once a year, and bet money on some of the races. The New Zealand woman was less inclined to marry during the 1970s than she had been in previous decades – a world-wide trend – but by 1981 the marriage rate was inching up again. But even if she does marry, she is less likely than her mother to have a child within the first or second year of marriage (although more than a fifth of New Zealand children are born outside of a marriage), and she will probably have fewer children. The New Zealand woman will quite likely work, at least part-time, while her children are still at school, and will return to the work-force after her children have grown.

Her children will enjoy a good education and, despite the modern spectre of entrenched unemployment, a good prospect of well-paid work for most of their lives. The type of person who originally came to New Zealand fostered the egalitarian concept, and did not accept the English class system as a model for their new homeland. Political leaders have generally boasted about their modest circumstances. The late Sir Keith Holyoake when he was Prime Minister between 1960 and 1972 was probably the most skilled practitioner – walking from his home to Parliament each morning, greeting other pedestrians along the way, answering his home telephone personally (he was listed in the directory) and dubbing himself "Kiwi Keith". But the voters loved it. The other popular figures who rose to be Prime Minister had similar backgrounds: Seddon was a "rough diamond" from the West Coast coal fields; Savage worked as a cellarman; Peter Fraser was a watersider; Walter Nash had been a commercial traveller at one time; Norman Kirk had been a stationary engine driver. The provision of universal free education, and the considerable financial assistance given to those who want to go on to university, has meant that all children born in New Zealand have the chance to make of their life what they want. More than anywhere else in the Western world, the New Zealander is unconcerned with the origins of his or her fellows. No one is trapped in a class system, nor prevented from fulfilling his or her ambition through lack of money.

One marked characteristic of New Zealanders is their passion to leave the country – most for a holiday abroad, but many to settle elsewhere. In 1980, there were nearly half a million temporary departures from the country – equivalent to almost a sixth of the nation's population. Young New Zealanders have traditionally gone abroad for a year or two to see the world before they settle into a career at home. England was once the main attraction, but the introduction of fierce restrictions on Commonwealth citizens has tarnished the attraction of the "Old Country", and now Australia has become a major destination.

Times of economic hardship have always brought outward migration from New Zealand. Between 1885 and 1892, 125,000 people left the country, with the holds of ships being filled with makeshift berths to accommodate all the passengers wanting to go. In the late 1970s the deteriorating economy led many to leave; between 1976 and 1980, the permanent departures almost doubled. A country of two or three million people can not offer the opportunities for the glittering prizes, and many of the most able have been among the departures. Famous New Zealanders have included writers who lived abroad such as Katherine Mansfield; cartoonist David Low; Lord Rutherford, who split the atom; Kiri te Kanawa, now one of the leading operatic sopranos in the world; Sir Edmund Hillary, conqueror of Mt Everest; Rowena Jackson, ballerina; a former British Ambassador to Mongolia; Joh Bjelke-Petersen, the Premier of the Australian State of Queensland.

Much of the success of New Zealanders abroad stems from their ability to turn their hands to a great many tasks. Domestic servants have never been widely used, even in Victorian times, so that self-reliance is part of the way of life. New Zealanders make repairs on their houses themselves (quite a few build their own homes) and, for many, Sunday morning is no longer set aside for church, but is the time to service the family motor car. By European standards, the New Zealander is a person who spends most of his leisure hours at home, or when socialising, does so in friends' homes. The cafe of Europe, or the corner pub in England, were never transplanted to the South Pacific. There has always been a marked puritan streak in the New Zealand way of life. The rampant drunkenness of the early decades led to the formation of women's temperance groups and during World War I the country came very close to enacting prohibition; instead the nation settled for the hotel bars to close at six in the evening, thus producing what became known as the "six o'clock swill", where thirsty New Zealanders poured into the the bars at the end of the day's work and drank as much, as quickly, as they could by the time the bells rang at six. It was not until the mid 1960s that this was repealed, and even then the bars stayed open only until ten o'clock. Before late closing, the sole outlet for social activity was the country dance or the coffee "bar" in the cities, a phenomenon of the post-war years when many of the earliest of these cafes were started by European migrants. The last decade has seen an incredible change. Restaurants have mushroomed in cities and towns throughout the country, but they are still largely the preserve of the wealthier New Zealander, or the younger single generation.

The restrictions, not to say greyness and boredom, of urban life have driven the men and women to outdoor activities, and sport and manliness have become part of the national creed. And, of all the sports, it is Rugby Union football which is still considered the national game. It was introduced into New Zealand in 1870 and blossomed as association football (soccer) was never able to do. The pinnacle of the sport is the All Blacks, the popular name for the national New Zealand team. The name is said to have originated during the 1905 tour of Britain when a printer, told that the entire side performed like backs, so swift were they, mistakenly turned out a sign which welcomed the "All Blacks", although it is

Richard John Seddon (1905), Prime Minister of New Zealand, 1893–1906. Removed from school at the age of twelve having proved a difficult and unpromising student, Richard John Seddon (1845–1906) worked on farms, foundries, gold-fields and as a store-owner, before winning a place on the Westland Provincial Council in 1874. In 1879, representing the Liberals, Seddon won the seat for Hokitika; fourteen years later he became Prime Minister of New Zealand, a position he held until 1906. (Schmidt Collection, Alexander Turnbull Library, Wellington.)

more likely that the black playing uniform was responsible. Although the traditional rugby rivals such as South Africa, Wales or the combined British team can always produce sold-out stadiums, at a local level the game has fiercely strong roots; in the winter months, every school playing field, every major sports park, and a great many country paddocks have the familier H-shaped goal posts at each end. Boys start playing at about the age of seven, and many men play on to the age of thirty. In the summer, cricket is the main spectator sport, although the New Zealand cricket team has never achieved the international reputation of the All Blacks, and only in 1983 scored its first-ever test match victory on English soil. Golf and lawn bowls may get little exposure on television and in the newspapers, but huge numbers of people play. Along with netball, they offer some of the few opportunities for New Zealand women to participate in sport.

Horse-racing is a curious mix in New Zealand. On the one hand New Zealand has more race meetings than days in the year. In the 1979–1980 racing year, the Minister of Internal Affairs licensed 489 days of racing (307 gallops, 182 trotting meetings) even though no race meetings are allowed on Sunday. On the other hand the Government maintains strict control on gambling and bans private bookmakers from all courses – the puritan streak again. And also a profitable streak, as gambling on horse-races brings the Treasury nearly $50 million in taxes. Race-meetings fill every Saturday and most weekdays of the year, and they can range from the high-stake events at the major courses, to the picnic meetings at small country courses like that at Omakau in Central Otago. The national racing administration has been trying for a number of years to amalgamate many of the smaller clubs, but local resistence has prevented most of these attempts. The major race-meetings are always occasions for the latest fashions, and thousands flock to courses such as Trentham, where the Wellington Racing Club is headquartered, to see not only the horses but the smartly dressed men and women.

New Zealand's rugged landscape and thousands of kilometres of coastline offer the chance for many other outdoor activities. Tramping in the many ranges of hills is extremely popular, and a network of huts is maintained through the hill and bush country. A more select number take up mountaineering. The Southern Alps provide a magnificent training ground for mountaineers, some of whom have attained world fame for their exploits, although the Alps regularly claim victims, both injuries and deaths, often as a result of quick and violent changes in the weather.

The forces of insulation, of being in a small country thousands of miles from anywhere, have resulted in a quite definite New Zealand accent. New Zealanders tend to feel that they speak something close to BBC-type English, that is, an accent-less speech – at least, until they go abroad. Even Australians can tell a New Zealander after a few sentences; just ask him to say "six" – it invariably sounds like "sux", leading one Australian wit to dub New Zealand the "land of the strangled vowel". Part of the problem may be that New Zealand schools, with a few honourable exceptions, have never bothered to teach children how to speak and project their speech, whereas so much vigour has been poured into the drilling of correct grammar in the written word. The Government-controlled radio and television services have traditionally set high standards of speech and diction, but this has not permeated into general New Zealand speech.

But if English has suffered, the Maori language has been battered in the mouths of the *pakeha,* particularly place names. The *pakeha* has never found the inclination to employ the rich vowel sounds of the Maori tongue, nor even to attempt to cope with the whole word if it is long. Thus the town north of Wellington called Paraparaumu becomes "para-param", the Hawke's Bay centre of Waipukurau is rendered "Wai-puk", while the former mining town of Kaitangata in Otago is sometimes just "Kai".

Like the Australians, the New Zealanders have produced their own words and slang expressions which are incomprehensible to those outside the country. "Dairy" is not only the place where cows are milked, it is also the corner shop which sells the bottled milk and other basic food necessities; to "pull your leg" means to playfully mislead you; a "cobber" is a good friend; a "walloper" is a policeman; the term "to bale up" means not just wool anymore, but to corner or confront someone; "a crib" is a South Island seaside cottage; "a dag" is a funny character, while "a hard case" has a slightly different meaning, implying more that the person may have a deal of gall or affrontery.

5. History

The first man, some part of the Polynesian race, landed in New Zealand – it is thought – about 100 years before William the Conqueror landed on the southern coast of England. When the first white man, the Dutchman Abel Tasman, found the coast in 1642, Charles the First of England and Scotland was on the throne; and when James Cook re-discovered and mapped the three islands of New Zealand, the American War of Independence was just seven years away. Such is the recent span of New Zealand's recorded history.

The little knowledge that we do have about those earliest settlers is sketchy. As close as possible, scholars have estimated that it was about 950 AD when man first arrived, although the main migrations of the people who came to be known as the Maori probably did not take place for a further three centuries. Theories that originally the Polynesians were descendants of Asian races remain theories. That they came by boat to New Zealand from the eastern part of Polynesia seems more certain, although whether this was by accident or design in the first instance is not known. Just how many migrations, or from how many islands, is not known either, so the term Maori can be applied only to the latter stages of their history in New Zealand when a common culture had evolved. Those who settled first are generally known now as "moa hunters", because they would have had to live off the land and sea before the subsequent migrations established the kumara and other plants in their new homeland.

The Polynesians had to adapt themselves to the new environment. Here there was snow and sleet, wind and rain, and cold that they would never have known in the tropical islands of Tahiti or from wherever it was they came. The crops ripened only once a year, not all year round as was the case in the islands. Cloaks and other garments made from flax and feathers were needed for the winter. Proper houses were built.

War was a constant factor in Maori life before European settlement, although it was more in the form of raid and skirmish than out and out major battles. Grievances were settled by raids and punishment; those who were not killed in the defeated party were often turned into slaves but even then slaves in Maori society were treated well by the standard of the time. They could even marry into their new tribe, and their children were not slaves. The Maori had an ordered society, where the system of *tapu* was evolved in order to provide a form of prohibition, whether of a burial ground, a tree that would be kept for canoe-building, or a crop that should not be used by members of the tribe.

The Polynesians eventually merged into one – the Maori – although they were divided within that culture by tribe. By the time of the first European contact, there was also a common Maori language, although it had quite distinct dialects. The language is closely related to those spoken in the Cook Islands, Hawaii and Tahiti – in fact, James Cook on his first voyage to New Zealand had a Tahitian to interpret between his crew and the Maori. Until the first Europeans began to settle in New Zealand, Maori was an unwritten language, but by 1815 the first book had been published in Maori by a member of the Church Missionary Society, Thomas Kendall. In 1844, a dictionary of Maori words was published.

The common language would have been reinforced by the frequent contacts between tribes. Maori society was reinforced by trade and exchange between tribes; the greenstone found only in the southern part of New Zealand was taken north, while the kumara from the warmer growing areas of the land were transported southwards. Gifts were exchanged between chiefs. This intricate pattern of communications between tribes and regions was conducted by means of walking or by canoe. A number of tracks developed, providing routes for those Maoris moving about the country.

For at least 700 years, the Polynesians had New Zealand to themselves, but in 1642 the first European intrusion took place. Just before Christmas of that year, the Dutch vessels *Heemskerck* and *Zeehaen* sighted the West Coast of the South Island, along which they sailed until turning into what is now Golden Bay, at the tip of the northern end of the South Island. The leader of this expedition, Abel Janszoon Tasman, was under orders from the Netherlands East Indies Company to search for the great southern continent which was wishfully believed to be waiting somewhere in the southern seas, beyond the discoveries of Europeans at that stage. Tasman sent a landing party to make contact with the brown-skinned men he saw from his ship. When the rowboat neared the Maoris, they attacked the Dutch and killed four of the sailors. Tasman named his only contact with the coast and the tribes it harboured, Murderers' Bay (changed to its present name after a later wave of white settlers felt that Tasman's name was not quite one with which they wished to live). He charted a little of the coast further north, named it Staten Landt – later changed to Nieuw Zeeland – and sailed away. For another 127 years no known European ship visited New Zealand. Tasman's discouraging report on his new discovery – that it offered little in the way of potential commerce – would have persuaded at least the Dutch not to waste any more time on the place.

It was left to the British naval captain, James Cook, in the vessel *Endeavour*, to re-discover the islands, to chart them and to demonstrate their potential. So successful were his series of three voyages of discovery that they were quickly followed by a succes-

Historic map of New Zealand, 1835.

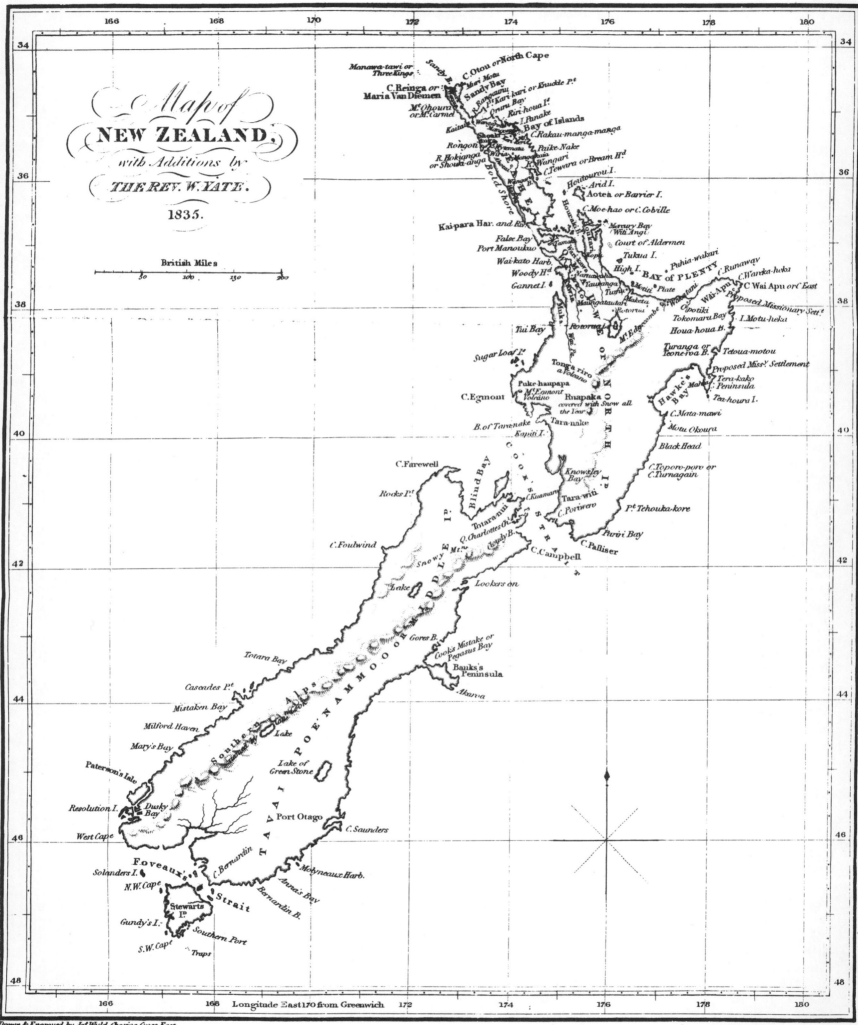

Map of
NEW ZEALAND,
with Additions by
THE REV. W. YATE.
1835.

Drawn & Engraved by Ja.s Wyld. Charing Cross. East

103

Page 105
Mansion House Bay, Kawau Island.

Page 106
Auckland Government House.
Government House, Auckland, was built in 1856. Soon after the signing of the Treaty of Waitangi, Governor Hobson moved his capital south to Auckland, which was not even a settlement of any shape then. The town grew rapidly, but in 1865 the capital was removed to the other end of the North Island, and Wellington became the centre of government from then on.

Page 107, above
Captain Cook statue.
Captain Cook's statue stands at Gisborne with Young Nick's Head in the background, the point where Cook's young crew member first sighted the coast of New Zealand.

Page 107, below
Lord Freyberg statue.
A statue to Lord Freyberg, who led New Zealand's army in Greece and other campaigns and then became the nation's Governor-General between 1946 and 1952.

Pages 108/109
Stone wall and farm, Otago Peninsula.
The Otago Peninsula forms one side of the Otago Harbour, at the top of which Dunedin is situated. It was an early farming settlement and many of the original stone walls still stand. A popular tourist outing with its winding roads, the area is particularly noted for the albatross colony at the harbour entrance.

Page 110
Cathedral Square, Christchurch.
Cathedral Square, at the heart of Christchurch, is now a peaceful pedestrian precinct and popular midday rendezvous point.

Page 111, above
Government building, Wellington.
The Government building at Wellington is believed to be the largest wooden building in the southern hemisphere. The foundation piles are totara, the frame is of Tasmanian stringybark and bluegum, and the weatherboards are four-centimetre-thick kauri. Until recently even the paving of the street was kauri coated with bitumen.

Page 111, below
Old St Paul's, Wellington.
Old St Paul's, Wellington, has a breath-taking wooden interior. This fine Gothic church, consecrated in 1866, has been superseded by a new cathedral.

Page 112, above
Treaty House, Waitangi.
The Treaty House at Waitangi is officially known as The Residency, for it was the dwelling, office and court of the Lieutenant-Governor. It was here, on the sweeping lawns overlooking the Bay of Islands, that the Treaty of Waitangi was presented and signed in 1840.

Page 112, below
Pompallier House, Russell.
Pompallier House, named after the Catholic bishop who founded his church's New Zealand mission, served as the printing house of the church. The house still holds the original printing presses.

Page 113
Larnach Castle, Otago Peninsula.
The most popular attraction on the Otago Peninsula is Larnach Castle, in the design of which R. A. Lawson played a major role. It was the home of William Larnach, leading businessman of Dunedin and a politician of national standing. Although Larnach was born in New South Wales, he had the Scottish taste for grandeur in stone. He committed suicide when faced with seemingly impossible financial problems.

Pages 114/115
Lake Tekapo and Church of the Good Shepherd.
The wildly beautiful Lake Tekapo is hidden in the Canterbury hinterland but reminiscent of the Scottish Highlands. The stone church on the bare headland has a clear glass window above the altar, framing the view of the lake and snow-capped mountain.

Page 116
Hop kiln, Dovedale.
Industrial archaeology: a long-disused hop kiln at Dovedale, Nelson.

sion of whalers, traders and missionaries (all of whom, incidentally, brought diseases against which the Maori had no immunity; between 1769 and 1840 it is believed the Maori population declined by more than forty thousand).

Cook's first sighting of New Zealand was from the east coast, near the present city of Gisborne. By circumnavigating New Zealand he was at last able to explode the myth of the great southern continent. The map which resulted from Cook's voyage around the coast was extraordinarily accurate; apart from a slight elongation of the South Island, the only major errors were the marking of Banks' Peninsula as an island, and Stewart Island as a peninsula. The botanists Solander and Banks provided the outside world with its first information about the profusion of birds and trees. So many of the present place names owe themselves to Cook's discovery, from Young Nick's Head near Gisborne in honour of the cabin boy who first sighted land, to Cape Turnagain to mark the spot on the Hawke's Bay coast where the *Endeavour* went about, to Cape Foulwind on the West Coast.

The *Endeavour* had been at sea more than thirteen months by the time young Nick sighted New Zealand. The first attempts by the British to find water and talk with the natives were as unsuccessful as Tasman's abortive effort, and Cook's party was several times compelled to fire upon the Maori parties and kill some of them. Not unnaturally, Cook was disappointed with his first landing in New Zealand, and bequeathed the name of Poverty Bay on the area. Other tribes were more amenable to bartering supplies, but the situation was always precarious: at Mercury Bay, one of the ship's officers shot a Maori who had snatched a piece of cloth and refused to part with his side of the bargain, and at what is now Thames, a young Maori was flogged for stealing an hour glass.

Cook then proceeded westwards around North Cape and down the other coast of Northland, along past Mt Egmont until he came to what he at first thought to be a huge bay, but was in fact Cook Strait, separating the North and South Islands. At Queen Charlotte's Sound, at the northern tip of Marlborough, he found a bay which offered timber and a stream in which he could careen his ship (turn it on one side) for cleaning and repair. This bay he named Ship Cove. It was during this time that Cook learned for the first time of the existence of cannabalism among the Maori.

After establishing that New Zealand consisted of at least two parts by sailing through Cook Strait and then northwards along the coast of the North Island to Cape Turnagain – which had been his southernmost point when he first sailed south from Poverty Bay – Cook then circumnavigated the South Island, naming many of the bays and islands, including Solander Island west of Foveaux Strait, after the expedition's official botanist. On the 1 April 1770, almost six months after first sighting land at Young Nick's Head, Cook bade farewell (for the moment) to New Zealand at the tip of the South Island he named Cape Farewell.

Several other explorers followed closely behind Cook: the

Frenchman De Surville who, unlike Cook, treated the Maori he met with brutality; his fellow countryman du Fresne; George Vancouver who had been on Cook's second voyage; and an Italian, Malaspina. The expedition of two ships led by du Fresne arrived in the Bay of Islands in 1772, and the crews set about being as friendly as possible to the Maori inhabitants. At first all went well, and the sailors were able to set out on their task of obtaining trees for new masts and replenishing supplies of food and water. But a number of unpleasant incidents occurred, culminating in an attack on a shore party led by du Fresne himself. It was only the investigations of a search party which uncovered the fate of the missing thirty men. They found the village of the local chief, Te Kuri, abandoned – except for the human remains which had been cooked and eaten, and a bloodstained shirt which they recognised as having belonged to their captain.

George Vancouver, by contrast, had a comparatively uneventful visit to the Fiordland area in 1791, the only threats being posed by the treacherous weather in that region. He carried out surveys which rounded off the work carried out by Cook. A little more than a year later two Spanish ships, under the command of the Italian Malaspina, were the first European vessels to enter Doubtful Sound, further to the north. The Spaniards did not know that in Dusky Bay a party of sealers had been at work for some months. It was the first of many parties left in New Zealand and the islands to the south, which were to lead to the virtual extermination of the seals.

By the turn of the century, the sealing parties had done their bloody work off the Australian coast, and the coast of New Zealand was their next target. The seals were clubbed to death, their skins cured and the blubber rendered down in trypots. The gang of men were left for several months, and then a ship was sent to collect them and their cargo. In 1806, one ship arrived in Sydney carrying 60,000 skins. They erected ramshackle camps of dwellings fashioned out of tents, flax and wood; they ate the bare rations given them, supplemented by seal meat, fish if they caught any, and native birds. Some of the longer-term camps established vegetable gardens. The foundation of the convict settlement at Sydney had made possible the exploitation of New Zealand and the southern seas.

The seals were almost gone by 1810 and, while the sealers turned their attention to the remaining colonies on Macquarie and Campbell islands, a new trade – that of whaling – was flourishing. The whalers concentrated their efforts at the Bay of Islands. Many of them were aboard American ships working out of Sydney, although seeking crews among the Maori tribes. The arrival of a succession of ships sparked off a considerable amount of violence along the New Zealand coast. Both sides were to blame, the Europeans because they were generally ignorant of Maori sensibilities and particularly of *tapu,* and they also stole from the Maori and molested the women; the Maori could also steal, and there were attacks on Europeans for a multitude of reasons. The

Shakespeare Head, Mercury Bay. Captain Cook sailed into Mercury Bay on 4 November 1769 and discovered one of the safest harbours he was to encounter on his journeys. Provisions were plentiful, and the ship's company enjoyed fresh water, black oyster-catchers, wild celery and fish provided by the Maori fishermen.

murder of du Fresne and his men in 1772 was followed by the massacre of the crew of the *Boyd* in 1809. The *Boyd* was bound for Whangaroa from Sydney to load timber. The crew numbered several Maori, one a chieftan, who during the voyage was flogged for a misdemeanour. When the *Boyd* dropped anchor, the captain and some of his crew were lured ashore and murdered. The Maori party then dressed in the sailors' clothes and boarded the ship and set about the crew and passengers. Four people survived; seventy were killed that night. Shortly after, a Sydney captain who was off New Zealand at the time, revenged the massacre with one of his own, attacking the *pa* he thought to be responsible and murdering many of the inhabitants.

The missionaries arrived when they were most needed. The types of European then frequenting the shores of New Zealand were generally rough, uncouth and violent. Missionary groups in London decided that it was time the Maori was protected from these poor types. In 1814 an Anglican mission was established at the Bay of Islands, and on Christmas Day the Christian gospel was first preached on New Zealand soil. Methodist and Roman Catholic missions soon followed. Within a decade, various mission stations had been established as far south as the Bay of Plenty. That first sermon was preached by Samuel Marsden, who had established a prosperous farm near Sydney. He was joined in the first mission by William Hall, John King and Thomas Kendall, although Marsden continued to see Sydney as his permanent home. None of his agents in New Zealand were trained clerics; all were artisans whose assignment was as much to teach the Maori craft as to convert them to Christianity.

Augustus Earle, visiting New Zealand in 1827, described Sunday in the Bay of Islands: "It was the custom of the Europeans to refrain from all kinds of work on the Sabbath; to shave, to dress

When Captain Cook anchored the *Resolution* in Dusky Bay in 1773, he sent officers out to kill a seal "which afforded us a fresh Meal". Two decades later a party of sealers arrived at the bay, and began the New Zealand-wide slaughter that was to continue into the early nineteenth century, leaving the seal colony decimated.

themselves in their best clothes; and if any of the missionaries came over, they went forth to meet them, and hear divine service. The natives, noticing that all this happened every seventh day, called it 'the *pakeha's tapu* day', and, strange to say, they also stopped working on that day . . . After a while we discovered that they had noticed that we generally lay longer in bed on a Sunday morning than any other, so they were up by the break of day, and had completed many hours' work before we made our appearance; but the moment one of us did appear the work was instantly let off. This showed more respect than we Europeans pay to any religious ceremony we do not understand."

The missionaries had mixed success in converting the Maori. The Anglicans were the most effective, partly because they were the most numerous, and because they had a head start. The missionaries tried to intercede where conflicts erupted between tribes; they tried to curb the worst excesses wrought by drink and the desire for the goods which Europeans brought. They urged the Maori to sobriety, thrift and hard work. But one missionary, William Yate, described in 1835 how he came upon one village and began to tell the natives about the message of Christianity, whereupon most walked away and the few who remained fell asleep. To add insult to injury, the Maoris demanded to be paid for listening. While the missionaries beseeched their tentative flock to avoid liquor, the busiest of the European settlements, Kororareka, was awash with alcohol. The whaling crews attracted Maori women aboard their ships with the promise of drink.

It was only a matter of time before the British Government had to take some steps toward establishing law and order in New Zealand, mainly to protect the Maori people. Their action was reluctant; they did not wish for any more colonial burdens, but the growing unruliness and the increasing trade made it inevitable. The British Parliament in 1817 and 1823 provided that the courts of New South Wales could try and punish British subjects for offences committed in New Zealand, but apart from the difficulty of enforcement, there were also plenty of French and Americans adding their contribution to the disruption and immorality of the new settlements. There was also the problem of fighting between Maori chiefs over women and land which, although it was nothing new to the native population, scandalised Marsden who felt it his duty to intercede. He realised that no centralised authority could be organised within the Maori population, as it was hardly likely that any chief would willingly cede his authority to another. The British took a major step toward complete involvement in 1832 by appointing a British Resident. James Busby did his best to restore order, but he was given minimal help from the Governor of New South Wales and his mission was doomed to humiliating failure.

By the 1820s, the Maori had begun to acquire muskets in substantial numbers. Chief Hongi Hika organised the Ngapuhi into huge war parties of two to three thousand men and raided the Waikato, Bay of Plenty and down the East Coast, butchering most of those whom he defeated. The chief of the Ngati-toa, Te

Samuel Marsden as a young man. Samuel Marsden became chaplain to the colony of New South Wales in Australia at the age of twenty-eight. By 1802 he had established a farm at Parramatta, at which he entertained the sons of Maori chiefs who had become keen travellers since the arrival of the first ships in New Zealand. In 1814, Marsden sailed across the Tasman and established New Zealand's first mission, fulfilling a life-long ambition. This was the first of seven lengthy visits, during which Marsden became the first European to explore the New Zealand interior.

Rauparaha, raided the Ngati-tahu in the South Island. He then laid siege to the Kaiapoi, near the present city of Christchurch, and with the aid of a treacherous white captain, lured one of the chiefs and his wife aboard and tortured them to death. The musket had transformed Maori fighting from raiding, where twenty or thirty men might be killed, into a bloodbath for whichever tribe lost.

While the British Government resisted being drawn into this antipodean imbroglio, Edward Gibbon Wakefield was trying to force its hand. Wakefield wanted a charter to colonise the country, and was the driving force behind the New Zealand Company, set up for that very purpose. Wakefield's theory, which held some sway in England at the time, was that land in the new colonies should not be priced too cheaply because if the land cost next-to-nothing, then it was worth next-to-nothing. What Wakefield did was to convince a section of British opinion that the colonies should be settled with some care.

In May 1839, the New Zealand Company despatched the vessel *Tory* to Port Nicholson under Colonel William Wakefield, Edward's brother. The Company stressed that the French were about to settle near Akaroa, although the French never had any intention of trying to annex the land. Some historians accept the Company's claim that it forced Britain to annex New Zealand, but the appointment of Busby and the growing British concern with the country had signalled the eventual annexation, Wakefield or not; it seems more likely that the New Zealand Company wanted to stake its claim before the archipelago became legally a British concern. Colonel Wakefield, upon landing in New Zealand, purchased 20 million acres in the Company's name. On 22 January 1840, the first of the Company's settlers arrived at Wellington.

By 1839, before the New Zealand Company entered the picture, there were already about 1000 British subjects living in New Zealand. In August of that year, Captain William Hobson was despatched by the British Government to negotiate with the Maori tribes so that they might accept the Queen's sovereignty over the entire land held by the tribes and to annex outright, if he saw fit, the South Island (which, a few years previously, that canny Australian squatter W. C. Wentworth had claimed to have purchased – along with the Stewart Island – for £200). On 5 February 1840, several hundred Maori gathered at Waitangi in the Bay of Islands to hear what Hobson had to say.

William Colenso, brother of the Bishop of Natal and printer, ornithologist and student of the Maori language as well as a missionary, wrote an account some years later of that day. The official party, which included Hobson, Busby and the Roman Catholic bishop, as well as the more plainly dressed Anglican clergy, were on a platform in the centre of the large tent erected for the purpose. In front of the platform, the chiefs and other Maoris stood, with white settlers and troops around the edge of the tent. "Tareha, chief of the Ngatirehia Tribe, rose, and with much of the usual national gesticulation, said 'No Governor for

Planting the British flag at Akaroa. In the 1830s there was some speculation that the French were planning to settle near Akaroa on the Banks Peninsula on the South Island. Though it is suggested that the New Zealand Company forced England to annex New Zealand in 1840, thereby thwarting any plans the French may have had and strengthening the Company's own position, several French colonial buildings survive to remind us of the early uncertain days.

me – for us Native men. We, we only are the chiefs, rulers. We will not be ruled over. What! thou a foreigner, up, and I down! Thou high, and I, Tareha, the great chief of the Ngapuhi tribes, low! No, no; never, never. I am jealous of thee; I am, and shall be, until thou and thy ship go away'. That was one of a number of speeches against the Treaty that day. One of the few to speak in favour was Tamati Waka Nene, chief of the Ngatihao. He turned to his fellow chiefs and said: 'Had you spoken thus in the old time, when the traders and grog-sellers came – had you turned them away, then you could well say to the Governor "Go back", and it would have been correct, straight; and I would also have said with you, "Go back"; – yes, we together as one man, one voice. But now, as things are, no, no, no. O Governor! sit. I, Tamati Waka, say to thee, sit. Sit thou here; dwell in our midst. Remain, do not go away'."

It was the crucial speech. The chiefs had to face the fact of European settlement which was gaining momentum, and that Hobson was the best chance they had of preserving their land and customs. Whether they were reassured, as Hobson shook each hand which signed the Treaty, with the words "We are now one people" is open to conjecture. About fifty chiefs signed on 6 February (with a total of 500 signatures after the Treaty had been taken around the country to other tribes). Three months later Hobson issued a proclamation which asserted the Queen's sovereignty over "the Southern Islands of New-Zealand, commonly called 'The Middle Island', and 'Stewart's Island'; and, also, the Island, commonly called 'The Northern Island', the same having been ceded in Sovereignty to Her Majesty."

Before long, there were disputes about just how much the Maori chiefs had ceded, but the dye was cast. New Zealand was British. The settlers could come, knowing they would be protected – at least in principle – by British law and justice. And come they did. By the end of the year there were 1700 Europeans settled in and about Wellington (by this time Hobson had decided to establish the capital at Auckland), although the initial land purchases by the New Zealand Company were reduced by the British authorities to about a tenth of that claimed. Large numbers of settlers were chosen because they would provide the labour and artisan skills judged to be needed.

Most of the first settlers in Wellington were English. They came ashore at Petone beach, the spot marked now by a large memorial, and the local Maoris helped them build rude shelters, but until they were finished most camped on the waterfront. After they had huts, the next task was to start clearing the forest. By 24 March 1840, just two months after the first settlers arrived, the Union Bank of Australia opened an office at Petone; a month later, the New Zealand Gazette was in business. Apart from the flour and other staples brought from England, the settlers relied on the Maori to supply fresh vegetables and fowl. The settlement even had its own clergyman who had walked and canoed overland from Auckland to minister to this small flock.

Tamati Waka Nene, chief of the Ngatihao, helped convince Maoris gathered at the Bay of Islands on 5 February 1840 that they should accept sovereignty and the terms Captain William Hobson was offering; the Treaty of Waitangi was signed on the following day.

The first settlement was called Britannia and laid out where Petone is today, although it was probably the most exposed part of the harbour, as can be verified by standing on Petone beach in a southerly gale. The problems of taming the Hutt Valley were confirmed when one member of the settlement took six days to get as far as the head of the valley. It was only a matter of time before the settlement was established where downtown Wellington is today; there was not so much flat land, but it was far more sheltered from the winds gusting up the harbour. The early plans called for grandiose proposals, including one for an inland harbour connected to the main harbour by canal; so it is today that the Basin Reserve was first named even though it ended up as the city's cricket ground rather than an inner dock, and the canal line which was to lead to it is a large grass strip running between Kent and Cambridge terraces. Lambton Quay, now quite high and dry, was then the new town's waterfront; land reclamation has produced much more flat land.

The centre of life in early Wellington was Barrett's Hotel, which survived in name until the last few years. It was in the public bar that the local citizens met after the day's work to talk about their common problems; it was here that any special dinners were held (and there seems to have been a plentiful supply of champagne in the very early days); and it was here that public meetings were organised and it even provided a chamber for the Wellington Provincial Council to hold its meetings. But there was still a considerable number of settlers at Petone, who found it easiest to travel to Wellington by boat across the harbour. Then, in 1855, as a result of an earthquake, a piece of land was formed, along which the Hutt motorway and the railway now run. Before that a road was in existence, but it was fairly rudimentary and narrow.

The basic necessities were the first priority at any of the new settlements. Dr Henry Weekes, who arrived at New Plymouth in 1841, reported that the first task upon reaching the beach was the erection of tents for the night. The next morning, a group of Maoris arrived at the site exchanging watermelon and potatoes for biscuits. Unlike Port Nicholson (Wellington), the site for the planned town was covered with fern and not forest. A week after the settlers arrived, they had their first taste of rain in New Zealand: "Heavy rain fell on the 7th and 8th [of April 1841] and as some had removed to their slender habitations rather prematurely, they and everything they had, were thoroughly drenched. Some of the women were glad to clothe themselves in any woollen garments they could obtain, and one who was dressed in a long-tailed coat over a flannel petticoat, with her feet in a large pair of nailed boots and a stick in her hand, reminded one – strange association! – of the late Princess Marie's statue of Joan of Arc. I have now put up a small panelled cottage brought with me, and find myself comparatively comfortable. The roof indeed admitted so much water at first as to oblige me to sleep under umbrellas; but a coating of thatch has made it quite watertight. No board roofs will of themselves stand the sun and heavy rain of New Zealand".

Treaty Monument, Bay of Islands. On 6 February 1840, shortly after the New Zealand Company had purchased 20 million acres, the Treaty of Waitangi was signed in the Bay of Islands by about fifty Maori chiefs, establishing the sovereignty of the Crown over the islands of New Zealand.

Page 125
Plimmer House, Wellington.
Plimmer House, a preserved wooden home in the centre of Wellington, sits uneasily amid modern office towers. It is now a fashionable restaurant.

Page 126, above
"Alberton", Auckland.
"Alberton" is one of Auckland's most historic houses, and a fine example of the decorated verandahs and balconies which superseded the earlier and simpler colonial architecture. The house was the home of a prominent land-owner and business-man, Allan Kerr Taylor, in whose family the home remained until bequeathed to the Historic Places Trust in 1972. It is now open to the public.

Page 126, below
Government Gardens, Rotorua.
For the older New Zealander bowls is the most popular sport. Here bowlers are set against the elegance of the Government Gardens at Rotorua which were designed to emulate the appeal of the European spa. Now the main building contains a museum and art gallery.

Page 127
Old houses, Tinakori Road, Wellington.

Page 128
Duart House, Havelock North.
Duart House at Havelock North is another example of the domestic architecture that was popular with the moneyed clas-ses. Havelock North has a population of 8500 and is near the city of Hastings, a town of substantial homes set among trees.

Page 129, above
House in Te Awe Awe Street, Palmerston North.
An early middle-class house common throughout New Zealand. This home at Palmerston North shows New Zealand's wooden architecture.

Page 129, below
Historic Norwegian building, Norsewood.
A house of Scandinavian-style architecture was built by Norwe-gians who were among the many immigrants to southern Hawke's Bay and northern Wairarapa. The immigrants paid their way by felling and milling the good totara timber in the forests.

Page 130, above
Hannah House, Wellington.

Page 130, below
Kemp House, Keri Keri.
The Bay of Islands, where the European first came in large numbers and where Governor Hobson established his first capi-tal, still contains many fine historic buildings. Kemp House is New Zealand's oldest surviving building, originating from 1821–1822.

Page 131
Waihemo Grange, 1863.

Page 132
Mission House, Waimate.
Mission House, Waimate North, was constructed by Maori workers for the Church Missionary Society in 1831–1832. It is furnished with mission period furniture.

Weekes and his fellow settlers soon discovered that the Maori living in Taranaki were good hands at a bargain. "A pig could be procured at first for a large blanket; but the price rapidly rose to two or more according to the quality, of which the natives were generally better judges than the Europeans... A man would come to your window and hold up a fish which after a little bargaining he would sell for a shilling; he would then produce from under his blanket a much finer one, which you think to be the last, and obtain for another shilling; when lo! another is produced finer than both! But a little experience of this sort made me feel them round carefully before I commenced fish-dealing."

Meanwhile, in Auckland the first homes were being built after Hobson had decided to establish his capital there, the timber coming initially from Tasmania. A solid bungalow cost about £2000. Life soon became established, as one Mrs Mathews described in reminiscences later written down: "The Governor and Mrs Hobson had taken up their abode at Government House, and there were many families now, besides the official circle. So there were visits to pay and receive, there were parties and balls, and a Philharmonic Society established of amateurs... We thought it right to take our part in these duties to Society, and aids to civilisation; but we were never so happy as when alone, and at home, reading or conversing, though always ready to give up these our favourite occupations, when the duties of hospitality required it". Life in tents or raupo huts was obviously unpleasant, but it was also inconvenient. Fires could not be lit inside them, so that when it was raining it was always a problem cooking. But by 1843, Auckland was starting to look like a town and shops and hotels went up alongside the houses which the settlers had now built themselves, and by now, too, local timber production was in full swing. The following year, the first brick building was finished. There was a simplicity about most of the buildings because the main need was to get them up as quickly as possible, so that the more intricate colonial architecture did not come until much later. Normally they were without even a verandah, and inside there were just a few rooms, and the only furniture available in the early years was that which the migrants brought with them on the ships. The Maori was there to provide food, but soon the settlers established market gardens and introduced sheep and cattle to provide more variety of meat. The children were initially taught at home, but gradually private schools were opened.

Those who went on to the land outside Auckland faced a far more primitive life-style. Home was a small timber shack of one room; the children had no time for schooling as they were needed to work on the land. Nor were there doctors, so that in case of injury or illness all that was available was a rudimentary form of first aid. However, there was usually a strong sense of community in the new rural settlements, as each family depended on others for help both in major tasks like felling trees and in emergencies.

While the settlers nibbled at the edges of the forests, a few more hardy souls explored the hinterland. At first, the missionaries set out into the bush to found new mission stations. Charles Heaphy, of the New Zealand Company, spent many years battling through the dense bush of the country exploring virgin regions. Another employee of the New Zealand Company, Dr Ernst Dieffenbach, set out at the end of 1839 to climb Mt Egmont, battling heavy scrub, pelting rain, rats and the reluctance of local Maori men to accompany him. In 1846, a surveyor, Thomas Brunner, decided to explore the interior south of Nelson in the hope of finding good farming land. His journey took eighteen months. It took him six months to follow the Buller River to its outlet where the town of Westport stands today, six months of driving, relentless rain, days without food, gorges and precipices which had to be climbed or walked around, rivers to be crossed by raft. The road trip today is 230 kilometres and can be covered in less than a day. He then forced a path down the West Coast, finding only more hostile country before re-tracing his steps to Nelson, arriving there partly paralysed and exhausted. Today, a town and a lake on the West Coast of the South Island bear his name.

While the Maori had been happy, by and large, to welcome the European and to supply food and other items, it was not long before the mounting *pakeha* pressure on the land bred fear and suspicion in the Maori mind. By 1856, there were 45,000 Europeans living in New Zealand. By this time George Grey, one of the major figures in New Zealand history, had been Governor. He was an autocrat, and determined to protect the Maori interests. But neither Grey nor his successor could halt the inexorable penetration of the land-hungry settler.

This pressure had proved a nightmare for Hobson, then his successor Robert Fitzroy (another naval captain); neither had the resources or the inclination to draw the line with the settlers. The appointment of Grey was an attempt by the Colonial Office in London, which was now responsible for the conduct of New Zealand's affairs (both European and Maori), to restore the standing of the position of governor in the eyes of both the settlers and the native population. Grey had appointed as head of the Native Land Purchase Department a Scotsman, Donald McLean. The Governor's idea was that McLean and his staff would buy up land from the Maori – in advance of European settlement – so that by the time the settlers arrived any conflict over ownership would have been resolved. Not unnaturally, McLean found it easier to deal with those Maori land-owners who were predisposed to sell, which only served to make those who resented the encroaching European frontier even more suspicious and nervous. It was not as if the British administration had no inkling of Maori frustration; Hone Heke in 1844 created a legend when he cut down the flagstaff at Kororareka and – less frequently remembered – then proceeded to set fire to the township.

The flashpoint was at Waitara, now a peaceful little town on the Taranaki coast, where McLean concluded an agreement with a minor chief for a block of land, when the acknowledged leader of the local Maori people, Wiremu Kingi, was opposed to the sale.

College Chapel, Auckland, in the 1880s. Bishop Selwyn, who spent a considerable period of his time in New Zealand at Waimate, gave a sermon in the College Chapel, Auckland, on the return from one of his lengthy journeys to the Melanesian islands that were included in his diocese.

Bishop George Augustus Selwyn (1809–1878) founded a string of mission stations throughout New Zealand. His travels around his diocese, which took him far into the Pacific and included New Zealand's outlying islands, and his vision and genius for organisation, make him one of the country's heroic figures. On his arrival in New Zealand in 1842, the Bishop established the Theological College of St John for the instruction of young men (both Maori and *pakeha*) for admission to holy orders; his house, in the grounds, is pictured here.

Kingi had a *pa* on the land, and substantial cultivations. McLean, with the support of the Governor Sir Thomas Gore Browne, was determined that the sale should go through regardless of the claim by Kingi that he had traditional right to some of the land involved in the purchase. The local settlers rushed to enlist in the militia, and then proceeded to invade the block of land and burn Kingi's *pa*. The Maori Wars had begun.

At first the Maori had the upper hand through sheer numbers in Taranaki, and they drove out most of the white settlers and burnt their houses. But the Maori tribes, though they would battle gallantly and fiercely on and off for another decade or more, were doomed to fail. Their ancient muskets and spears were no match for the cannon and modern rifle possessed by the British troops and the local militia. The fact that historians this century have almost unanimously declared that the Maori were, at the least, wronged, only goes to add an element of tragedy to the whole episode. Grey was recalled from Cape Town to once again take up the position of Governor in the hope that he could bring peace. But the situation was too far gone for that.

The Maori fought to the end. At a small village of Orakau, one of the few remembered individual battles took place. The tribes of the King Country, loyal to the Maori King Tawhiao, made a stand against the white soldiers. No one has described it better than William Pember Reeves, one of New Zealand's greatest political figures, writing in 1898: "Some three hundred Maori were shut up in entrenchments at a place called Orakau. Without food, except for a few raw potatoes; without water; pounded at by our artillery, and under a hail of rifle bullets and handgrenades; unsuccessfully assaulted no less than five times – and they held out for three days, though completely surrounded. General Cameron (the Imperial Commander) humanely sent a flag of truce inviting them to surrender honorably. To this they made the ever-famous reply, 'Enough! We fight right on, for ever!' (Heoi ano! Ka whawhai tonu, ake, ake, ake.) Then the General offered to let the women come out, and the answer was, 'The women will fight as well as we'. At length, on the afternoon on the third day, the garrison assembling in a body charged at quick march right through the English lines, fairly jumping (according to one account) over the heads of the men of the Fortieth Regiment as they lay behind a bank. So unexpected and amazing was their charge that they would have got away with but slight loss had they not, when outside the lines, been headed and confronted by a force of colonial rangers and cavalry. Half of them fell; the remainder, including the celebrated war-chief Rewi, got clear away. The earthworks and the victory remained with us, but the glory of the engagement lay with those whose message of 'Ake, ake, ake' will never be forgotten in New Zealand." One of the most extraordinary sidelights of the wars was the cult of the Hauhau. It was, to say the least, a travesty of Christianity, but its most persuasive (if, in the final outcome, least plausible) tenet was that believers could invoke powers which would turn bullets away.

Hone Heke. Under the leadership of Hone Heke and Kawiti, the dissatisfaction of the northern Maoris flared into warfare in the middle of the nineteenth century. The British forces soon learned that the Maori was a formidable fighter and an outstanding military tactician.

By 1870, the wars were, for the most part, over. The main victims were the Maori. In 1840, their population had been estimated at between 115,000 and 160,000. By 1870, there were only 37,000 Maori left. The Government set about confiscating the land of those Maoris who it held responsible for the conflict. In all, although much of the land belonged to Maori people who had little involvement in the wars, 1.25 million hectares (3 million acres) were taken. The criterion seems to have been whether the land was good for farming rather than the bellicosity of the tribe possessing it.

While the wars raged in the North Island, the South Island was undergoing a quite different experience: the gold rushes. The first major discovery was near the present Otago town of Lawrence. There, in 1861, Gabriel Read found gold. Dunedin, the port of entry for the Otago goldfields, changed from the restrained Scottish settlement of 12,000 to a licentious 60,000 people. Four years later, gold was struck in Westland and thousands of miners poured in from Australia and from the Otago diggings. At its zenith, Hokitika had ninety-nine hotels to absorb most of the earnings of the miners. Read's discovery brought 14,000 miners before the end of the year. The next year, the target of the gold fever shifted up the Clutha River near Cromwell where two Californian miners, Hartley and Riley, had discovered substantial deposits. More and more finds were made: first at Bannockburn, then the Nevis, eventually in the Arrow and Shotover rivers; then it was on to St Bathans, Cambrians, Naseby.

The easiest gold was extracted simply by shovel, dish and cradle. However, much of the gold was contained within massive deposits of quartz, and quite different methods were required. For these, intricate and long water races were built to bring water to the deposits; to them were added quartz crushers, huge river dredges, waterwheels, even the diverting of streams and rivers.

The hardships were great for those who sought a quick fortune. Many died in harsh winters, especially when sudden changes of weather caught men far away from shelter (see Chapter One). The roads from Dunedin, such as they were, were impassable in winter in the early stages of the gold rush. Food and other supplies were often not to be had. When they were, the prices were usually exorbitant. A handful of timber – always needed for working at the fields – could cost £5, while cartage from Dunedin was charged at the rate of £120 a ton.

In comparison with the lawlessness and unrest on the Australian and Californian fields, the New Zealand diggings were peaceful. An armed constabulary was soon employed throughout the fields by the Government, and they successfully guarded the gold shipments to Dunedin. One of the few major incidents occurred near the West Coast diggings. In 1866 five miners were found murdered on the Maungatapu trail which led to Nelson. The killers, to become known as the Burgess-Kelly gang, were quickly apprehended. Three of the gang were hung, the fourth was imprisoned for life.

King Tawhiao. The tribes of the King Country, the followers of the Maori King Tawhiao, made a stand against the New Zealand soldiers at Orakau, a battle which has since become an important part of New Zealand history.

Charge of the New Zealand Cavalry at the battle of Orakau. Cavalry was of little use in the Maori-European Wars owing to the nature of the country and the tactics of the Maoris.

Rewi Maniapoto (c. 1815–1894). Rewi Maniapoto, a descendant of Hoturoa and a chief in his own right, became prominent in the "King" movement of the 1850s in which loyalty to the Maori King Tawhiao was observed. Maniapoto is probably best-remembered for his courageous stand during the Maori Wars in 1864 at Orakau, where a *pa* had been built as a show of confidence that the Maori could continue the war. Although running out of ammunition and water, the Maoris refused to surrender when General Cameron, impressed with the defenders' courage, offered a flag of truce. Cameron and his men eventually captured an outer part of the main *pa*, and the Maoris made their escape, although with heavy casualties.

The Otago fields were still being developed when gold was found on the West Coast. The year after the discovery, the West Coast was exporting more than two million pounds of gold. (Over the period af 100 years, more than fifty billion dollars worth of gold was exported from New Zealand, and as late as 1979 gold production in New Zealand was still more than $2 million in value.) Reeves was a contemporary of that great son of the goldfields, Richard John Seddon, one of New Zealand's greatest premiers. Seddon left a wonderful description of the transformation which overtook the West Coast: "On a strip of sand-bank between the dank bush and the bar-bound mouth of the Hokitika River a mushroom city sprang up, starting into a bustling life of cheerful rashness and great expectation. In 1864 a few tents were pitched on the place; in 1865, one of the largest towns in New Zealand was to be seen. Wood and canvas were the building materials – the wood unseasoned pine, smelling fresh and resinous at first, anon shrinking, warping and entailing cracked walls, creaking doors, and rattling window-sashes. Every second building was a grog-shanty, where liquor, more or less fiery, was retailed at a shilling a glass, and the traveller might hire a blanket and a soft plank on the floor for 3s a night. Under a rainfall of more than 100 inches a year, tracks became sloughs before they could be turned into streets and roads. All the rivers on the coast were bar-bound. Food and supplies came by sea, and many were the coasting-craft which broke their backs crossing the bars or which ended their working-life on shoals. Yet when hundreds of adventurers were willing to pay £5 apiece for the twelve hours' passage from Nelson, high rates of insurance did not deter ship-owners". Little remains of these settlements simply because their creation was so quick and improvised. Of Charleston on the West Coast, where a substantial shack and tent town once rose, only the substantial wooden hotel survived to modern times; in Nelson, the aptly named Canvastown practically disappeared as quickly as it grew. The miners who populated the fields at Central Otago, the West Coast, Nelson and the Coromandel came from many lands, but the one race which stood apart was the Chinese. They came to New Zealand as labourers and were allowed to work only the poor land, usually the tailings which had already been turned over for gold by the European miners. Although they posed no threat to the livelihood of the other miners, great resentment existed toward them, and Seddon largely built his early political career on trying to prevent any more Chinese workers entering New Zealand, although they were never physically persecuted as was the case on the Australian diggings. Today, one can wander around cemeteries in Central Otago and find many Chinese gravestones, even though they are usually set quite apart from the European graves. Many of the Chinese were shipped back to their homeland when they died; in 1902, the ship *Ventnor*, bound from Wellington to Hongkong with the remains of 489 Chinese, struck a reef off Taranaki and sank, killing some of the elderly Chinese accompanying the caskets.

But although the gold discoveries had some temporary effect on the nation's fortunes, and certainly around the diggings (the West Coast was a blank on the economic map before gold was found; by the end of the 1860s, a quarter of the European population of the country was in Otago), the long-term effect was not all that great. The number of unemployed was high, and communications between the different provinces were appalling apart from shipping.

Enter Julius Vogel. Vogel was a man of huge energy, who had dabbled in journalism and financial speculation. In Dunedin, he had started a daily newspaper, but it was there he became involved in politics, first in the Provincial Council, then in the national Parliament (which after 1865 was moved to Wellington). In 1870, he was Treasurer, faced with the problems of a stagnant economy and unemployment, both of which had resulted in declining immigration. Vogel believed that road and rail development would open up more land for settlement. The provinces could not provide the funds; they were saddled with debt, so it was the role of the central Government.

Over ten years, more than £20 million was borrowed. While the public debt quadrupled in that time, on the positive side was the doubling of the population to near half a million. Christchurch and Invercargill were linked by the South Island Main Trunk Railway via Dunedin, and railways spread out over the land. Before Vogel, the provinces had begun laying railways, but three different gauges existed and the Southland Provincial Council built its first line with wooden rails. Under the 1872 Railways Act, the one narrow gauge was imposed and lines authorised to New Plymouth, Wanganui, Foxton, Napier, Wellington, Picton, Nelson, Westport, Greymouth and Lyttelton as well as the Main Trunk to Invercargill.

New Zealand's economy was in doldrums for many of the thirty years between 1865 and 1895. Gold provided some relief, while Vogel's public works policies eased the unemployment situation, although the greatest benefit was to those who speculated in land affected by the various projects. But the event which really changed New Zealand's whole direction was refrigeration.

In February 1882, the sailing ship *Dunedin* left Port Chalmers with a shipment of mutton and lamb. The meat had come from the Totara Estate near Oamaru, and been railed to Port Chalmers on the Main Trunk line which had been completed as a result of Vogel's policies. Until this first shipment of frozen meat, which arrived in London in excellent condition ninety-eight days later, most of the farms were given over to wheat or wool, and much of the land was locked up by a small number of owners. New Zealand produced far too much meat for its own needs, and much stock was boiled down for tallow simply because there was no one to eat it. In Europe, at the time, there was no such meat glut. It was the perfect equation. And while there suddenly existed an outlet for all that surplus meat, the advent of refrigeration made possible the export of butter and cheese, hitherto nascent industries. By 1892, the effect of refrigeration on the economy was felt not only by the

Port Chalmers, 1880s. In 1844 Maori leaders assembled at Port Chalmers, originally known as Koputai, to sign a deed which allowed their land to be bought; five years later settlers' houses hugged the shoreline. In 1882, Port Chalmers was on the Main Trunk Line and was the scene of the first New Zealand shipment of frozen meat to England.

farmers but in the country towns which now had processing industries to offer employment. In that year more than a hundred butter and cheese factories were in operation, and twenty-one meat-freezing works.

At the beginning of 1891 the Conservative Government resigned, its place taken by the Liberal Party. Where refrigeration changed the economy, the Liberals, first under John Ballance and then Richard John Seddon, set in train reforms which transformed New Zealand into the social laboratory of the world.

And not before time. The poor had no assistance other than from inadequate private charities; the hospital system was disorganised; the pay and conditions for the urban worker were miserable. William Pember Reeves, who became Minister of Labour, pushed ahead with far-reaching reforms, including laws which prohibited payment of wages in any form other than money, giving workers the right to seek damages when they were injured through defective machinery, a Factories Act which established minimum conditions in which people worked, and the restriction of the working week for women and boys to forty-eight hours. Another act made employers pay manual workers on a weekly basis, but the Conservatives opposed a move to provide shop assistants with a lunch break. The most innovative of all Reeves' legislation was the Industrial Conciliation and Arbitration Act, which was the first legislation in the world to introduce a system of compulsory arbitration by the State in industrial disputes. Seddon, who was Minister of Mines until Ballance died, brought down legislation to improve safety and working conditions, and prohibit the employment in the mines of boys under thirteen.

When gold was discovered in 1861 at Gabriel's Gully in Otago, the nearby port of Dunedin became a wealthy and prosperous city. Thousands of diggers poured through the previously restrained Scottish town, swelling the normal population from 12,000 to 60,000. This view shows Dunedin in 1865, the year after gold was discovered in Westland, and illustrates the prosperity the city was enjoying at the time. Though the gold ran out, the boom of the 1860s had established Dunedin, and carried it through into the twentieth century as one of New Zealand's most beautiful cities. (Alexander Turnbull Library, Wellington.)

Page 141
Auckland Domain Glasshouse.
A tropical glasshouse in Auckland's Domain parkland, situated near the city centre.

Pages 142/143
Waitaki Boys High School, Oamaru.
Waitaki Boys High School, a fine example of Otago stone architecture, was opened in 1883 and was fashioned from the limestone widely used in Oamaru buildings.

Page 144, above
Polo players at Hamilton.
Page 144, below
The hunt.
The sporting heritage of England established by the first European settlers is evident in the popularity of polo and hunting in New Zealand. The polo teams compete with the best in the world, while hunt clubs pursue hares and other game rather than the traditional fox that has never been introduced into New Zealand.

Page 145
Packers Arms.
Bushwalkers gather for a drink at an old hotel, the Packers Arms.

Pages 146/147
Dunedin city in the early morning.
Dunedin, historic city of the south. In the 1860s Dunedin became the financial centre of the nation with the help of the wealth from the goldfields. It is still known as a city of "old money".

Page 148
Queen Street, Auckland.
Most New Zealanders live in the major cities even though it is a predominantly agricultural country. Auckland is the largest city, seen here looking up from the docks along Queen Street, the main shopping centre. Also noticeable in this photograph is the number of cars – there is one to every 2.4 people. The result is that public transport has been downgraded to the extent that railway services have been abandoned over vast parts of New Zealand, with the threat, at the time of writing, that all long-distance rail services would be withdrawn. The enormous cost to New Zealand of imported oil together with the promotion of road transport seem, to the outside observer, incompatible.

The other reformer was John McKenzie, the Minister of Lands. His father had been evicted from a croft in the Scottish Highlands, and was described by Reeves as "a gigantic Gael, in grim earnest in the cause of closer settlement". He declared war on the land monopolists – many of whom had acquired their holdings by dubious methods – and furthered the cause of the small holder. His first move was a Land Tax, which was aimed at the larger properties; one of them, the 16,000-hectare Cheviot property in Canterbury, was broken up for small farms as a result. Further acts provided for compulsory State purchase of large estates and for leasehold tenure, while the Treasurer, Joseph Ward (who was to succeed Seddon as Premier) introduced a law to allow the State to provide loan money for new land settlers.

Whereas women in Britain did not get the vote until after the Great War, their New Zealand counterparts received it in 1893 – the first in the world. A few years later, women were granted near equality with men in divorce proceedings, and a family maintenance law was passed to protect the rights of women and children.

The 1898 Old Age Pensions Act, which Seddon had to ram through the House of Representatives, was meagre. It provided that a weekly sum of 6s 11d (around sixty-nine cents) should be paid to those who were over sixty years of age, had lived in New Zealand for twenty-five years, led a sober and reputable life and had not a deserted spouse or child; there were also clauses covering criminal records and personal property. Possibly the worst aspect was that the would-be pensioner had to substantiate his or her claim before a magistrate's court.

However, although it was hardly a generous measure by modern standards, the significance of the Old Age Pension of 1898 was that it accepted the State's role in caring for its people. It is a role which is accepted to the full today, and has removed from the average New Zealander the fear that poverty, injury and ill-health would bring with them total destitution, as was so often the case in nations which had no such provisions. The social welfare state was greatly advanced after 1935 when Labour came to power and took up where Seddon left off, and each Government since then has strengthened and consolidated it. A national superannuation scheme has supplanted the former old age pension, while the accident compensation scheme removes the need for costly litigation to establish claims for injuries. New Zealand's pioneering and trail-blazing in the field of social welfare is one of the shining achievements of its modern history.

New Zealand has had internal responsible self-government since 1856. In 1907, with Ward as Premier, it was given Dominion status, which added no real powers to the Government in Wellington but did serve to give the country a specific political status. Although New Zealand did begin to exercise its powers (such as joining the League of Nations as a full independent member after the Great War), it was not until 1947 that it achieved full autonomy from Britain when the Fraser administration adopted the Statute of Westminster, by which the British Parliament made possible for the Dominions to adopt full sovereignty as independent nations. There was always a reluctance to cut the apron strings from Mother Britain.

Dominion status did nothing to alter the country's great feeling of affection for Britain, as was displayed in the ready rush to arms to defend the Empire in both world wars. The Premier, or Prime Minister as he was now known, was William Massey when war broke out in 1914. Not having a majority in the House of Representatives at the election held soon after war was declared, he offered to take the Liberals into his Reform administration and, thus, a National Government was formed.

In 1914, New Zealand's population was 1.14 million. During the war years, 100,000 men were sent to serve overseas. Sixteen and a half thousand – a sixth – were killed. (This was not the first occasion upon which New Zealanders had laid down their lives for Imperial interests; 6000 of them volunteered to fight the Boers in South Africa between 1899 and 1902.) Total casualties, dead and wounded, amounted to 58,000 New Zealanders. Belgium, with seven times more people, had 13,000 killed – and Belgium was one of the battlegrounds.

The first action of the war was the occupation of German Samoa, which was accomplished without fighting, the Germans at Apia fully realising that they could not put up any reasonable resistance. Two months later, the main body of troops left for Egypt, to ready themselves (along with the Australians) for the landing at Gallipoli. The coals of this battle have been raked over many times, and the shortcomings of the British military planning and execution clearly documented, but that does nothing to detract from the immense courage and bravery displayed by the fighting men of Australia and New Zealand in that campaign. Their task was impossible; but from April 1915 until December of that year, the Anzacs (as they came to be called) captured and held precarious beach-heads against the Turkish forces. Both Australia and New Zealand observe the day of the landings as a national holiday, a day of remembrance for all their men who died in war. A decade previously, New Zealand had declined to join the Australian Federation, preferring instead to go its own way, but the "spirit of Gallipoli" cemented a relationship between the two countries which remains to this day.

After the Gallipoli débâcle, the New Zealanders were moved to the French theatre, to the mud and death of Verdun, Flers, Ypres and Bapaume, among others. The war cost the young Dominion more than the flower of its manhood; the public debt more than doubled to over £200 million.

A socialist Labour Government was no less prepared to stand by Britain's side in 1939, even though some of its ministers had opposed New Zealand's participation in the 1914–1918 conflict. In this case, however, socialist ministers could unite against the fascist menace, and Japan's entry into the war made the threat all the more immediate. New Zealand soldiers, before the entry of Japan, were involved in the defence of Crete and Greece, and then the crucial campaigns against Rommel in North Africa. Again New Zealand sent 100,000 men away and this time the losses were only slightly less horrific; more than 11,000 men never returned home.

The New Zealanders fought hard in the defence of Greece, with the Maori Battalion being involved in some particularly heavy fighting against German forces. After the collapse of the Greek Army, the New Zealanders were withdrawn to the Mediterranean island of Crete, where their commander Major-General Bernard Freyberg was in command of the island's defence. Again the New Zealand forces had their backs against the wall and put up a stern defence against the Nazi invaders, but, just as in Greece, the aggressors were in far superior numbers and the Royal Navy was called in to evacuate the troops. After being re-formed in Egypt, the New Zealand Division was thrown into the North African campaign, suffering several heavy reverses, but eventually taking a major role in the pivotal Battle of Alamein. Then they fought the length of Italy, including the murderous and bitter fighting at the Battle of Cassino.

In the Pacific, New Zealand's greatest fear was that the Imperial Japanese forces should reach and take Fiji, which would provide a staging point for a Japanese invasion of New Zealand. A brigade group was rushed to Fiji as soon as it was assembled. The defeat of the British in Singapore proved a great blow to New Zealand morale, and the impact was all the more devastating because they now realised that this defeat (and the sinking of the British capital ships *Repulse* and *Prince of Wales*) meant that Britain could no longer offer any protection whatsoever.

On the other hand, the Americans could help – and did. In May 1942, the first American forces arrived in New Zealand. It was the beginning of a political and military co-operation which continues to the present, first through the South-East Asia Treaty Organisation (now defunct) and then the thriving Anzus agreement with Australia as the third member.

New Zealanders served in other theatres with distinction: many joined the Royal Air Force and a considerable number of Kiwis flew in the Battle of Britain. In naval warfare, New Zealand's greatest moment was when its light cruiser *Achilles* fought so heroically in the Battle of the River Plate against the German pocket battleship *Graf Spee*.

While its men were fighting abroad, the New Zealand economy was mobilised for the war effort. Able-bodied men who were not in the armed forces were called to the Home Guard which, in view of the potential Japanese threat, was given high priority. Thousands of women joined the Women's War Service Auxiliary, apart from the 10,000 women who joined the three services. One of the country's crucial contributions to the Allied war effort was the massive quantities of food produced, both for shipment to Britain and for the US forces in the Pacific. Over the period of the war, New Zealand shipped more than 3 million tonnes of butter, cheese and meat to the beleaguered British.

What was more amazing for what was predominantly a rural-based economy was the mobilisation of industry. Linen flax was not only planted and harvested, but seventeen processing factories were set up. The US forces were supplied with buildings of all types, wharves, ammunition from bombs to rifle shells, naval vessels from minesweepers to tugs, aeroplane parts, and all sorts of military clothing.

This unprecedented national effort was made possible, in part, by the presence of a Labour Government, whose substantial majority gave them the mandate to regulate the economy. Labour had come to power for the first time in 1935 charged with restoring New Zealand after the Great Depression.

The impact of the Depression was greatest when the prices of rural exports collapsed – 40 per cent in two years. Imports, consequently, were halved. Farmers were ruined when the prices they received for their products failed to pay the mortgages and other costs; all those who depended on the sale of imports, from watersiders to shopkeepers, were faced with shrinking work. The Reform Government, like its overseas counterparts, faced up to the problem by cutting spending – living within its income – which only made unemployment worse. The domino effect was in full swing, until in 1932 there were about 100,000 men unemployed. Relief work was the Government's only answer, and men were sent out to makeshift camps to perform back-breaking tasks for pitiful amounts of money. Holes were dug and filled in again. Swamps were drained, roads built with massed human labour. There were riots in Dunedin and shop windows were broken, while in Auckland a police baton used on one protest marcher sparked off a night of rioting and looting in the Queen City.

It was inevitable that Labour, the one party which had not been tarnished with the Depression, should win the 1935 elections, now seen as one of the watershed events in New Zealand history. They captured fifty-five of the eighty seats in the House of Representatives. Michael Joseph Savage was Prime Minister; Peter Fraser, an ex-watersider was the real force in the party, while Walter Nash, an ex-commercial traveller from Kidderminster in England, became Minister of Finance. Both Fraser and Nash in their turn would serve as Prime Minister, but they would never re-capture the spirit of those early years of Labour, when Seddon's torch was picked up and carried.

Labour threw itself with energy into the task, first restoring pay cuts and lifting relief work payments. Various parts of the economy, such as radio broadcasting, were placed under direct State control. Dairy farmers, whose electoral support had helped Labour win a number of parliamentary seats, were given a guaranteed price for their product. The working week was reduced to forty hours, and compulsory unionism introduced. Education was given high priority with teachers' colleges being reopened, and many new schools built. Factory legislation was tightened up. In 1937, malnutrition in children was attacked by a scheme which provided each schoolchild with a half-pint of milk each school day.

Michael Joseph Savage. (Gordon Burt Collection, Alexander Turnbull Library, Wellington.)

A Department of Housing Construction was set up to buy land, build houses and prepare them for occupation; by 1940, two-thirds of the houses being constructed were built by the State, and then let out at minimal rentals to those families whose housing was inadequate or who could not afford to buy a house. Prime Minister Savage helped carry furniture into the first house completed under this project. The momentous Social Security Act of 1938 increased pensions and family allowances, and for the first time there was established a national health service, making health care almost totally free. In 1946, a further major step forward took place when the family benefit, which had been subject to a strict means test, was made available to every child in the country – the mother receiving 10s a week for each child (the second Labour Government 1957–1960 made it possible to capitalise the benefit, that is take it in a lump sum for the value of sixteen years' worth, for a house deposit). Labour, with its four Maori members of Parliament, was also active in improving the lot of the Maori people, with efforts being made to improve housing and farming. And so New Zealand entered the modern era a much better place for its people than could have been imagined even twenty or thirty years earlier, and certainly well in advance of most other nations.

This dedication to "the quest for security", as one historian termed it, has been followed by every subsequent Government, although some have been more enthusiastic than others. At times public housing construction has been slowed down; and school milk was abolished to save money. But overall, the Savage-Fraser-Nash social fabric is intact. However, now that New Zealand's pioneering efforts have been overhauled by several other nations, it may not seem such an achievement to the new generations who take it all for granted. Historian Keith Sinclair has called it the greatest political achievement in New Zealand's history. Nothing has ever matched it – and probably nothing ever will.

Government House, Auckland. Founded in 1840 by Captain William Hobson, Auckland was the capital of New Zealand until 1865 when the government was moved to Wellington. The wooden Government House was completed in 1855 during the governorship of Colonel Gore Browne.

6. Relics of History

New Zealand is lucky that its extant historic buildings, sites and other relics have survived. Until the last few decades, the people were more interested in the future than the past. Buildings were pulled down without too much thought, Maori sites were ploughed under and historic areas such as the Otago goldfields were either vandalised or had any movable relic stolen.

Fortunately, the growing interest in and consciousness of the nation's history, both before and after the arrival of Europeans, has led to the preservation and restoration of much of what remains. It is surprising that so much, in fact, has survived. As far as buildings go, wood was used widely in the early days, most notably on the magnificent Government buildings in Wellington – the largest wooden structure in the southern hemisphere. Decay and fire account for the destruction of many of the wooden buildings, but there is still a rich variety of structures which are peculiarly New Zealand: the simple and elegant early houses in the Bay of Islands which recall the first white missionaries and administrators, the superb wooden houses of Wellington, the grand homes of the runholders on the big sheep stations, the simple and functional farm buildings. While much stone and brick was used, there was never the aristocracy as in Europe to build palaces and castles. The grand buildings are either churches, those built for Government, for big companies or for men who had deluded themselves to think that they could replicate the baronial style, such as William Larnach whose "castle" near Dunedin has been restored.

Not only were there not the major stone structures, but the wooden buildings and other relics had to contend with New Zealand's climate. The dryer climates of North Auckland, Nelson and Central Otago favoured the survival of places of historic interest. In other areas, particularly the West Coast of the South Island, the high rainfall not only rotted what was left behind, but meant that the thick bush soon sprang up and covered anything which did not rot.

While the European builder tended to seek simplicity, no such charge could be levelled at Maori architecture. Many of the highly decorated and carved buildings are of comparatively recent origin, but they employ techniques and designs which faithfully follow the older forms. The buildings stand all over the North Island, with some in the South, notably at Otakou on Otago Harbour. One of the most splendid examples of the heights which

Carved gateway of an old *pa*. Maori dwellings were gathered in villages which, for defence purposes, were often placed on a hill and surrounded by high fences with ditches and earthen walls so as to make a great stronghold called a *pa*. Gateways were intricately carved and stood as an impressive entrance to the village.

Mask of hard wood finely carved with *moko*. The back of the mask is hollowed out to fit the face, and eyes, nose, and mouth are pierced through. There are pierced lugs at the sides and one on the top.

Maori art has reached is in the meeting house at Waitangi, next to the Treaty House which stands as a memorial to the signing of the Treaty of Waitangi. The meeting house was finished in 1940, New Zealand's Centennial Year, and accommodates carved figures supporting the centre poles and an intricate mixture of carving and painting on the walls and ceiling. The Maori people have frequently employed tukutuku, which are decorative wall panels fashioned with reeds and thin wooden slats laced together with strips of flax grass in the form of lattice work. These patterns can take many forms, even within the one building, and can be seen to great effect in some of the larger meeting houses such as Poho o Rawiri, the meeting house for the Maori people of the Gisborne district. The marae, the courtyard of the village, is the centre of Maori life and the meeting house its court. This Gisborne house is regarded as one of the finest built during the 1920s.

Some maraes have become extensive settlements, most notably Turangawaewae at Ngaruawahia, home of the present Maori queen, Dame Te Atairangikaahu. Its centrepiece is the meeting house, Mahinaarangi, the great house for those tribes which form the King Movement. Thirteen carvers worked on the meeting house. It is decorated in the finest traditions of Maori artistry, yet before the resurgence of Maoritanga this century it was possible to detect European influences creeping into Maori art. The Rongopai meeting house, built in the 1880s, has painted decorations, but no carving. The traditional patterns are there, but human figures, previously non-existant in Maori art, are represented as a westerner would paint them. Wi Pere, a Maori member of Parliament, is shown wearing a waistcoat and jacket, striped trousers and spurs on his boots.

Historic Maori sites have been less generously treated than their buildings. The widespread sowing of pasture over the landscape of New Zealand has meant that the plough inevitably destroyed many sites of considerable historic significance and interest. In Tolaga Bay, north of Gisborne, giant discing in 1983 destroyed the remains of kumara storage pits that were part of an old Maori *pa*. Some have survived and demonstrate the earthworks involved; at Papamoa on Tauranga Harbour the site of Wharo *pa* is wonderfully preserved. Built on the top of a small hill, it is still possible to see the terraces which were built below the *pa* itself, which would have once been lined with stakes and would have provided several lines of defence in the case of attack by another tribe. In the Tongariro National Park, the remains of a Maori fort have been preserved as a reminder of the Maori Wars.

Of European structures, the oldest are to be found – naturally – in the Bay of Islands region. Many of the buildings still in existence date back to those earliest days, and several are now preserved by the New Zealand Historic Places Trust. They are not old in European terms, but are significant in that they represent the first signs of European influence in New Zealand. The oldest surviving building is Kemp House at Keri Keri. It was built for New Zealand's first clergyman, the Reverend John Butler, in

Page 157
Turuturumokai *pa,* Taranaki.
Many remnants of early Maori settlement have been obliterated by the plough, but of the Maori *pa* (villages) which survive one of the most interesting is that at Turuturumokai in Taranaki. It was built about 400 years ago when inter-tribal warfare was particularly common in this part of New Zealand. Its battlements were pressed into use again in 1868 during the Maori Wars.

Page 158
Hayes Engineering Works, Oturehua.
Hayes Engineering Works at Oturehua in Central Otago are housed in mud brick and corrugated iron buildings, with much of the turn-of-the-century plant still in working order.

Page 159, above
Soldiers' club, Marlborough.
Each farming district had its hall, which was either in the nearest village or stood in a field by itself. This was the centre of the community, where meetings were held and marriage receptions and Saturday night dances were the main social outlets. The Soldiers' Club in Marlborough is an example of the simple and functional architecture adopted for these buildings.

Page 159, below
Matamata Historic Tower.
The Refuge Tower at Matamata was built by Josiah Firth during the Kingite War of the 1860s, as a place of refuge against Maori attack.

Page 160, above
Huka village, Taupo.
Huka village at Taupo where craftsmen display the skills once part of the settler's life.

Page 160, middle
"Cobblestones" stable, Greytown.
The "Cobblestones" stable is located in Greytown (in the Wairarapa Valley north of Wellington), one of the country's most attractive towns with its many old cottages. These stables were used by the Cobb and Co. coaches.

Page 160, below
Old coal-mine near Greymouth.
The high rainfall and resurgent bush has meant that little has remained of early mining and settlement. One of the more recent reminders of the glorious past is this tiny coal-mine near Greymouth. Coal-mining is largely operated by the State, but on the West Coast a number of small private mines flourished until recent times.

Page 161
Galloway Station, stable.
This stable at Galloway Station in Otago shows how the early farmers followed the miners in using the schist rock for building. The province had few trees in this region, and it was hideously expensive to transport lumber from Dunedin.

Page 162
Keri Keri and stone store.

The stone store at Keri Keri, the oldest surviving stone building in New Zealand, is maintained by the Historic Places Trust and still operates as a general store.

Page 163
Chapel of St Stephen, Parnell.
St Stephen's, Parnell, is in a part of Auckland where the early upper classes lived. Many prominent early Aucklanders, including the city's first Anglican bishop, are buried in its grounds.

Page 164, above left
Maori carving, Te Kaha Meeting House.
This Maori carving at Te Kaha in the Bay of Plenty shows the typical tattooing seen by the first European visitors. The tattoos were made by a sharp bone and mallet and the recipient usually needed several days of rest to recover from the ordeal.

Page 164, above right
Meeting House, Waitangi.
The Meeting House at Waitangi was built by the Maori people to commemorate the centenary of the signing of the Treaty of Waitangi. It contains carvings executed by several tribes as their contribution to the project. The Meeting House is used each year to celebrate the signing of the Treaty on 6 February 1840, Waitangi Day now being a national holiday.

Page 164, below
Meeting House, Ohinemutu.
Ohinemutu village is now part of the city of Rotorua, although it preceded the city by some decades. The Meeting House was built as recently as 1943 but it contains some of the decorations from its predecessor which depict legends going back to the first Polynesian settlers in New Zealand.

Page 165
Maori Whare, Keri Keri village.
A Maori village at Keri Keri has been restored as a display attraction.

Page 166, above
Nursery, "Broadgreen", Nelson.
Page 166, below
Kitchen, "Broadgreen", Nelson.
Wood was popular with the settlers at Nelson. One of the best examples of a colonial gentleman's home is "Broadgreen", now open to the public. It was built by Edmund Buxton, who had land in Canterbury and a business in Nelson.

Page 167.
Historic sod cottage near Balclutha.
At Lowells Flat in South Otago the local community has restored this pioneer cottage as a reminder of the way of life of the first settlers in the area. This cottage is typical of thousands which dotted the southern farmlands.

Page 168
Otago Boys High School, Dunedin.
Otago Boys High School dates from 1884 and was the work of the area's leading architect, R. A. Lawson, who designed many of the city's major buildings.

selves, not a great deal remains due to the fact that most buildings – like on the West Coast – were made of wood, although the Thames School of Mines survives even though it is an unpretentious wooden building. Although the School is a museum piece today, the other engineering industries are still clinging on. The most notable is the factory of A. and G. Price. The company was attracted to Thames in 1871 by the obvious opportunities to manufacture mining machinery, and a range of equipment for the then flourishing sawmilling. As those industries declined, the Price company switched to building steam locomotives for New Zealand Railways – 123 altogether – as well as steam, petrol and battery locomotives for private industry and bush tramways. Today the company is still an integral part of Thames – and a living piece of history as well.

But, for substantial relics of the gold rushes, the place to go is Central Otago in the South Island. Here again the hotels have survived in considerable numbers, although the architecture is quite distinct from Thames. The most famous pub is possibly the Vulcan at St Bathans, once a thriving gold town but now a hamlet with a population of less than twenty. The Vulcan was built with mud brick and, until the interior was unfortunately modernised in recent years, it had only four guest bedrooms and a dining room with one large table around which all the guests sat. Its Lilliputian dimensions were matched by a tiny tin church a few metres away.

But the more usual building material on the goldfields was stone, of which there was ample supply in the largely treeless interior of Otago. The hills abound with the ruins of very rudimentary stone cottages. The walls have survived remarkably well on most, while the roofs, being made of less permanent materials, are the main victims of the elements.

Most of the towns of Central Otago maintain some of the air of the old days. Of them, Clyde is particularly redolent with its narrow main street lined with a number of old buildings, including the Dunstan Hotel, the post office and museum. Cromwell, although it has preserved some of its older sites, will lose most of its historic associations when an artificial lake behind a major new hydro-electric dam covers much of the area. Arrowtown, which stands on one edge of the picturesque Arrow River, has maintained its old main street with a magnificent row of preserved miners' cottages; some of the old commercial buildings have been redeveloped and each day Arrowtown is overwhelmed by bus and car loads of tourists.

Nevertheless, some quiet backwaters remain where one can stand and sense the noise and bustle of the old gold days. Central Otago has many sunny, totally windless days which are perfect for creating the atmosphere of peace and introspection. Quite off the beaten track is the tiny settlement of Ophir where a beautiful post office made from schist stone, to which you drive down a narrow road and across the river by an elegant suspension bridge, still opens each morning for business. Further up the road is Oturehua, once known as Rough Ridge, where one of the few un-

The mission house at Waimate (Bay of Islands) is the only surviving house of the first inland mission. Three houses, dating from 1831, originally comprised the mission at Te Waimate, twenty-four kilometres from the Bay. The extant structure, which became Bishop Selwyn's "palace" in 1842, was altered in the 1870s, but the hipped roof and dormer windows have been restored.

modernised general stores remains in business. The town also has the Hayes Engineering Works which was built to supply machinery to a nearby flour mill and to local farmers. The factory is accommodated in mud brick and corrugated iron buildings while the machinery, although looking like a Heath Robinson invention, is still in good working order.

Outside the townships there are many reminders of the gold boom. Along the hills are the stone culverts which were built as water races, while river banks have large slices sluiced out of them. Pieces of rusting machinery, usually only those too heavy for the weekend souvenir hunter, lie all over the province. The more adventurous fossicker may find blocked-up mine entrances in the gorges. Tailings are everywhere, from the moonscape at Gabriel's Gully near Lawrence, where the first strike was made, to the deposits of gravel left by the massive river dredges at Earnscleugh.

Farm buildings offer another splendid range of early New Zealand buildings. The nearest New Zealand ever came to an aristocracy, or at least the landed gentry, was on the Canterbury and North Otago plains. Many of the earliest families which established large land holdings are today still leading citizens and prominent members of the community. Less often remembered is the way many of the runholders acquired their land in the first place; they, and their counterparts in Wairarapa, Hawke's Bay, devised dubious methods, but it was the squatters of Canterbury who raised it to a fine art.

No wonder the landholders could afford to build themselves rural mansions. Stories abound of the privileged families with their servants (who received back copies of *The Times* by sea and then ironed one copy each day and laid it on the breakfast table just as if their master were in London) and the large numbers of underpaid farm labourers who toiled to perpetuate the owner's fortune. But they at least built with taste, so that Canterbury still has today not only the substantial and elegant homes, but aesthetically pleasing farm buildings, from simple but huge shearing sheds to stone woolsheds.

In Otago, farmers followed the example of the miner in using schist, rock which is easily split to form flat surfaces, to build their homes and outbuildings, the buildings on the Galloway run being among the finest examples. In North Otago, a different form of rock was used. In the peaceful and prosperous town of Oamaru there are many examples of fine structures fashioned from limestone, or Oamaru stone as it is more popularly known. Actually, for a town of just 13,000 people it is a little amazing that such magnificent buildings should be found. Among them are the Bank of New South Wales complete with Corinthian columns, the old post office which dates from 1864, and the National Bank which was designed by the man responsible for so many of Dunedin's finest structures, R. A. Lawson. The streets around the old port are a magical precinct of utilitarian but elegant commercial buildings in limestone, while the court house of 1883, with its classical design and fluted columns, is arguably Oamaru's finest building. Just outside the town limestone was used to dramatic effect in Waitaki Boys High School, one of the most highly regarded secondary schools in New Zealand. Limestone was also highly favoured in Dunedin, particularly by Lawson. He used it there on First Church, for the outer veneer, the foundations being of Port Chalmers stone. The church stands on what was a hill, levelled in the early days in order to make the inner town flatter, the rubble going to harbour reclamation. Because it was the first major financial centre in New Zealand, Dunedin became a substantial-looking city from its early days.

Many of New Zealand's major companies were founded here, including National Insurance, Cadbury and National Mortgage. It was not until well into the twentieth century that many other large companies felt it necessary to move away to Wellington or Auckland. The city centre is the Octagon, dominated by a statue of Robert Burns, as is fitting for such a Scottish city, while around the perimeter much of the sykline has changed. But on the upper side is the stunning St Paul's Cathedral, and the Town Hall.

Dunedin is a city of fine stone buildings. Apart from its churches, many of the older commercial structures still stand. Near the main post office is the ANZ Bank building, with its striking Corinthian columns. The facade was saved from demolition by a huge public outcry some years ago, and the bank built a new interior behind it. No such threat, fortunately, has faced the Railway Station, regarded as one of the finest in the southern hemisphere. Although it now sees only two passenger trains a day – and their future is in doubt – the station remains a monument to the time when it was regarded as important that travel be provided with some elegance and comfort. It is a magnificent and imposing stone structure, and is full of delightful surprises inside, with a mosaic tiled entrance foyer featuring a steam engine, and a wrought iron balcony above.

Out of town, on the Otago Peninsula which forms one side of Dunedin's harbour, one can drive past old farm buildings and the stone walls so common in Scotland, to Larnach Castle, one of the most ornate and ambitious buildings built by private means in New Zealand. The castle has had its ups and downs this century, at one stage falling into serious disrepair, but has now been restored to much of its former glory, the owners having managed to get back much of the house's furniture that was scattered after Larnach's death. The interior has also been partly restored to its original state. Larnach was a man of many talents; he was a prominent national politician, serving as Minister of Public Works and Railways in one government, Minister of Mines in another. He was a noted businessman in Dunedin's early days but his life ended tragically. He committed suicide in 1898 in a parliamentary committee room after the collapse of the Colonial Bank. The bank, which he had helped form, found itself in serious financial difficulties and he spent a good deal of his own money trying to rescue it. The castle itself is on four levels and covers 4000 square

Knox Church, Dunedin. The Presbyterian Church still dominates the religious life of the city, settled in 1848 by the Lay Association of the Free Church of Scotland (later the Otago Association).

metres. The entrance steps are flanked by lions, and from the superb stone exterior one moves into an interior with its kauri, oak, teak and mahogany timbering. One ceiling alone is the product of more than six years' work by carvers.

Stone is widely used in Christchurch, too, although in a much more restrained way than in Dunedin. The centrepoint of Christchurch is the Square with the Cathedral Church looking as if it had been moved, stone by stone, from an English town. Fortunately, a number of the older buildings in Cathedral Square have been retained and that, plus the closing off of much of the area to motor cars, has provided a wonderful inner-city precinct. Included among the buildings is the United Services Hotel that, with its Italianate facade, has preserved an old-world air; its high ceiling in the dining room, and the staff dressed in black and white, make for one of the more genteel meeting places in this placid city. Just a few metres away is the post office built in 1879 and now an integral part of the Square's architecture.

If stone was the building material of Dunedin and Christchurch, for Wellington it was wood. In the earthquakes of 1848 many brick and clay homes were badly damaged, so that it became extremely popular to use wood which was less likely to collapse. The Government buildings in Lambton Quay, across the road from the Parliament buildings, are the grandest examples of the use of wood.

Wellington abounds in wonderful examples of homes in the older parts of the city. Twenty years ago Thorndon, the first area of settlement, was a delight. Street after street of elegant old wooden houses stood peacefully with only the odd motor car to disturb the air. The suburb had a powerful neighbourhood spirit, many people having lived there all their lives. But, unfortunately, Thorndon has been plundered. A huge motorway was carved through its middle leaving what was left under the pall of urban decay as residents moved out and many of the houses were converted to rented accommodation. Other buildings were demolished for offices or blocks of modern apartments. All that said, one can still see some houses which have been lovingly tended. There are a few grand homes, including the one in which Katherine Mansfield was born, but the main interest in Thorndon is the way in which this largely working-class neighbourhood was constructed on steep slopes, with narrow alley-type streets and steps. What is particularly interesting is that most of the quite considerable problems of building on such a difficult landscape were solved not by architects, but by builders. It was usual for a builder to put up many of the houses in one area, so that it was a matter of gradually improving the designs as they went from house to house.

Much of Wellington has changed. In 1950 it was a city of three-storey commercial buildings, most of them narrow and crammed together, all with corrugated iron roofs. Now the central city is a cluster of huge concrete towers. But in Thorndon it is still possible to remember what it all used to be like.

Wellington, c.1888. The first emigrant ships reached Port Nicholson in January 1840 and the beautiful harbour was soon lined with warehouses, shops and hotels. Big houses were built on the hillsides near Mount Victoria and small wooden cottages lined the narrow streets. An 1880s account described Wellington thus: "As a capital city Wellington is not likely to impress the stranger. Its streets are narrow and tortuous, the footpaths of proportionately contracted width, and the buildings of all sizes and designs, and principally of wood and galvanised iron. Some years ago nothing more durable than timber was used, for the very reason that the prevalence of earthquakes has made people afraid to build with brick or stone. That dread, however, is vanished owing to extended immunity from such alarms, and within the last decade many substantial buildings have been reared at considerable cost."

7. The Political and Economic Systems

New Zealanders have never had a lack of government. Take, for example, the Hutt Valley, the satellite city of the capital, Wellington. In the early 1960s, this fast-growing dormitory had a population of less than 100,000 people. To administer its affairs, apart from the central Government in Wellington itself, the people of the Hutt had three borough councils and one city council; one county council; three boards to control fire services; one electric power and gas board; one river board; one harbour board and one hospital board (shared with Wellington); one milk board; one drainage board; and one underground water authority. Some of these boards were appointed, but the majority were elected, making local body election time in New Zealand a trial in patience and detail for the voter. It was no wonder that, in the early 1960s, the Government set up an inquiry into local government in the Hutt Valley to try to make it more streamlined and rational; nor was it any wonder that each proposal which involved amalgamation or abolition was fought to the end.

The New Zealander has always been keen to maintain control of his affairs on a strictly parochial basis, which is no bad thing. It makes sense that, in a small borough, all the councillors are familiar with the people for whom they administer, that they know the corner which needs a set of traffic lights. This way the council is not run by an army of administrators who are remote from the populace with only a monthly council meeting to ratify their decisions. Yet, on the other hand, there has never been any pressure to erect a network of checks and balances on the central Government. The political party which has a majority in the House of Representatives can, in theory, do what it likes. There is no written constitution, no one parliament can bind another, and the head of state, the Governor-General, would never dare oppose his Government (when the Governor-General of Australia did just that in 1975, he unwittingly ensured that no one would try that again). Until 1950, New Zealand had an Upper House, but the Government of the day was able to abolish it with little trouble – the Prime Minister, Sidney Holland, simply appointed a "suicide squad" of twenty-six new members to vote the Legislative Council, and their new jobs, out of existence. When, in 1875, the central Government tired of the provincial system – even though the provinces had their own elected assemblies and controlled such important matters as land sales, public works and education – it was simply a matter of passing the

Residence of Sir George Grey on the island of Kawau. Grey retired into private life here after his second term of Governor, although he was to enter politics in 1875. Kawau, comprising 5052 acres and situated in Kiuriki Gulf, some thirty-five kilometres north of Auckland, was a storehouse of innumerable curiosities, ranging from rare and important books and manuscripts to oil paintings of great value.

Sir George Grey (1812–1898) was Governor of New Zealand between 1845 and 1853 and again from 1861 to 1867. During his first years as Governor he was able to suppress Maori rebellions in the Bay of Islands and near Wellington, reconciling the local chiefs in the process in order to buy enough land for the immediate needs of the colonists.

appropriate statute through the central Parliament. Even the rights of the people to vote can be altered by the Government of the day; the Electoral Act of 1956 consolidated all the electoral legislation built up over the years, and contains a number of reserved clauses (such as those containing universal suffrage) which may not be changed by less than a 75 per cent vote in Parliament. The weakness of the Act is that, in the view of most constitutional lawyers, the clause which requires the 75 per cent majority could itself be repealed by a simple majority in the House of Representatives. Fortunately, New Zealand governments have never felt the urge to fiddle with the electoral system; when the Holyoake Government felt that the term of the Parliament should be four not three years, it submitted the matter to a national referendum, and was defeated.

New Zealand's Parliament meets when called by the Prime Minister, and there is no fixed date when this should be. To overcome the problem of not always having Parliament in session to pass legislation, the succeeding governments have given themselves vast powers of government by regulation. These regulations are issued by the Executive Council, which is the Cabinet chaired by the Governor-General. Normally, the regulations issued ensure the smooth running of the country, providing ministers with the flexibility to cope with unforeseen circumstances. But they can also be employed to intervene in such a way that, if it were done by Act of Parliament, would provoke vociferous opposition. The Public Safety Conservation Act had been passed in 1932 to allow the then Government the right to invoke emergency powers to control Depression riots, but then the Act's provisions were used in 1939 when the Labour Government imposed wartime restrictions far more repressive and severe than even Britain's, and again in 1951 by the Holland administration to fight the striking waterside workers. In 1942 and 1943 several publications were closed down, while the editor of the Manawatu *Times* was prosecuted for writing about industrial strife. In the 1951 strike, the National Government used the 1932 Act to promulgate regulations which made it illegal to refuse to work overtime (that is, work paid at a higher rate beyond the lawful forty-hour week), to display signs insulting to others or encouraging anyone to strike. These regulations allowed police to enter premises without a warrant while the Government gave itself the power to seize union funds. The 1951 waterfront strike still evokes bitter memories in New Zealand, but it seems clear that the Government of the time acted with scant regard for legal precedent. In 1960, the Labour Government amended the 1932 Act to ensure that Parliament could be called together within seven days of the emergency provisions being implemented.

The formation of the first European-type government, under Hobson, was covered in an earlier chapter, as was the establishment of the General Assembly in 1852, and the creation of the provinces. British common law is recognised by the courts, and the principles of habeas corpus and other basic rights evolved in

Page 177
Parliament buildings, Wellington.
Parliament buildings, Wellington. The older stone building houses the two chambers of the Parliament. The House of Representatives is a close copy of the British House of Commons, although smaller, where members of the Government and Opposition face each other. Close by is the Legislative Council chamber; the council was abolished in 1950 and since then the chamber has been used for a variety of functions, including conferences.

Page 178, above left
Whitebaiting, Hokitika River.
Bringing in the catch at a whitebait fishery on the Hokitika River.

Page 178, above right
Oyster farming, Bay of Islands.
Oyster farming, Bay of Islands. The cultivation of oysters is a relatively recent development. Traditionally New Zealanders have eaten Bluff oysters dredged from the sea floor in Foveaux Strait which separates the South and Stewart islands. Now rock oyster farming is a fast-growing industry with developing markets in Singapore, Hong Kong and the Pacific Islands.

Page 178, below
Fishing boats, Gisborne.
Gisborne, along with Nelson, Auckland, Manukau, Timaru, Tauranga and Greymouth, is one of the main fishing ports in New Zealand. However, because most of the fleet is made up of small boats, fishermen operate from practically every port and many settlements along the coast which have no shipping other than the local fishing boats. Much of the wet fish goes to supply local customers, while rock lobsters supply an important export market in the United States.

Page 179
Kapuni gas field and Mount Egmont.
Kapuni gas field is seen with Mount Egmont pictured behind. Kapuni was a small village in southern Taranaki until natural gas was discovered. Now gas from the area is piped to several major cities in the North Island where it has supplanted coal gas.

Pages 180/181
Chateau Tongariro and Mount Ruapehu.
Chateau Tongariro, a luxury hotel providing accommodation close to the ski slopes and thermal attractions, is situated in the 5000-hectare Tongariro National Park. Within its boundary, the Park includes Mount Ngauruhoe, New Zealand's most active volcano.

Page 182, above
Timber worker, Ruatapu mill.
Along the roads of the central North Island there is a constant stream of massive trucks carrying logs to the mills. In the 1990s huge new areas of exotic forests will come into production and, because of the problem of moving the logs by road, several new railway lines may be required.

Page 182, middle
Farming, Riwaka.
Across the river from Motueka is the picturesque township of Riwaka; which is the centre for hop research in New Zealand. Nearly half the annual hop crop is exported, West Germany and the United States being the main customers.

Page 182, below
Maraetai Dam and Mangakino.
Maraetai Dam is pictured with the supporting township of Mangakino in the background. The mighty Waikato River, 354 kilometres in length, rises at Lake Taupo and passes through nine hydro-electric power stations. Maraetai was opened in 1954 and it can produce up to 180,000 kilowatts of electricity.

Page 183
Sheep muster, Lillybank, Mount Erebus.
A common sight in New Zealand: a sheep muster at Lillybank near Mount Erebus. There are twenty sheep for every human in New Zealand, and sheep remain a mainspring of the country's economy.

Page 184
Wellington Club, Wellington.
The fancifully designed Wellington Club is found in New Zealands's capital city. In the classic colonial building which preceded it much of the nation's history was written by the powerful politicians and financiers of the nineteenth century.

English and Scottish law are upheld. Freedom of speech is guaranteed by the adoption of the 1688 Bill of Rights.

Because communications were so poor in the early days, the only effective way to govern New Zealand was considered to be through provincial administrations. Governor Grey defined six provinces – Auckland, New Plymouth, Wellington, Nelson, Canterbury and Otago. Later, the growth in population led to the hiving off for four more provinces – Westland, Marlborough and Southland in the South Island, Hawke's Bay in the North. However, the move by the General Assembly to the more centrally-located site of Wellington, the improved shipping services and the telegraph undermined the former arguments for provincial governments. The head of each province was the Provincial Council which in turn was overseen by a Superintendent; these controlled land sales, immigration, harbours, education and hospitals. The provincial governments were abolished in 1876, and since then the country has been governed from Wellington with local bodies providing a second tier of government.

The head of state is the Governor-General, representative of the monarch. Elizabeth II of the United Kingdom is monarch, but is now vested separately with the New Zealand crown making her Queen of New Zealand. The Governor-General fulfils the functions Her Majesty carries out in the British political system, except that the Governor-General is appointed on the recommendation of the New Zealand Government and serves a fixed term. It is now a convention that the appointment is given to a New Zealander rather than, as was the case until after World War II, a Briton of aristocratic background or military achievement.

The Parliament consists of the House of Representatives, the Legislative Council having been abolished for the generally agreed reason that it served no purpose. Its members were appointed for seven years by the Prime Minister, so that by the time Labour had been in power for fourteen years from 1935 to 1949, the incoming National Government was faced with an Upper House full of Labour Party stalwarts.

For many decades, the House of Representatives was made up of eighty members, but in 1965 the number of seats allocated to the South Island was set at twenty-five, a move designed to dispel southern fears that the increasing population of the north would mean a loss of electorates south of Cook Strait. The formula now provides for the number of parliamentarians to increase to meet the rising population in the North Island, so that at the 1981 election there were ninety-two members elected. Four electorates are allocated for the Maori population, although there are provisions for people of Maori descent to choose to be included in a general electorate. The boundaries of the general electorates are redrawn after each five-yearly population census by the Representation Commission, which consists of senior public servants and a member representing both the Government and Opposition in the House of Representatives. It is possible to lodge an appeal once the new electorates are announced. The system is accepted as the fairest possible, and New Zealand is fortunately free of the gerrymandering still common in other democratic nations.

New Zealand has had a remarkably stable Government. Since the end of World War II, only one administration has failed to serve its full three-year term, and that was in 1951 when Prime Minister Holland saw the chance to increase his majority on the issue of the waterfront strike. The last period of instability was between 1928 and 1931 when a minority United Government existed, first, on Labour support and, second, on Reform votes until it was driven into coalition with the latter. Between 1957 and 1960, Walter Nash's Labour Government had an effective majority of one seat, but superb organisation in the House resulted in the Government never losing a vote when the House divided along party lines.

The small size of the New Zealand Parliament means that each minister takes on several portfolios; if the departments were handed out singly, just about every Government MP would be in Cabinet. At the time of writing, for example, the Prime Minister, Sir Robert Muldoon, also held the portfolios of Finance, Audit and the Security Intelligence Service. Another minister held Social Welfare, Public Trust Office and the Government Printing Office; the Minister for Maori Affairs is also Minister of Police; the Minister of Customs also had to worry about being Minister in Charge of the Government Life Insurance Office, the State Insurance Office, the Earthquake and War Damage Commission, with the role of Associate Minister of Trade and Industry being his responsibility as well.

The number of portfolios illustrates the pivotal role of the State in the daily life of the New Zealander. If he wants to travel, he can choose the State railway, which also operates many of the bus routes, or fly the State airline; if he wants to be a writer, he stands a good chance of getting a State grant; all his television and the majority of his radio entertainment is supplied by State-owned organisations; the State will offer him life and property insurance, draw up his will and administer his estate after death; it will provide him with a house if he is a low-income earner; it operates ships to carry his exports around the world; it runs the hotel he stays in if he goes to one of the major tourist resorts.

No one wants to have it any other way. The various political parties will occasionally tinker, but the continuing stability is largely due to the lack of major ideological differences between the parties. They would, naturally, deny that. But the evidence of the post-war period is that "fine-tuning" is as far as anyone is prepared to go. And this consensus is due largely to the homogeneity of the New Zealand population. The system is a two-party one, conservative and reformist although in different guises, and with the differences being greater or lesser depending on the state of the economy.

The present National Party, which has dominated the Government benches in the House of Representatives in the last three decades, is the embodiment of the conservative side. The long

Sir Joseph Ward (1856–1930) was Liberal Prime Minister from 1906 to 1911. During his lifetime he was principally known for his ability as a finance minister. He was a fluent and quick speaker and able to dazzle his audiences with masses of figures.

Liberal ministry from 1891 until 1912 revived the conservative movement in the guise of the Reform Party which in turn held office until 1928. Then it was the turn of the Liberals again, although this time they were called the United Party. The leader was the aging Sir Joseph Ward, who had held office as Liberal Prime Minister from 1906 to 1911. His last political victory was the product of a glorious mistake. On the platform during the campaign in 1928, he meant to promise that his party, if elected, would borrow £7 million for each of the next ten years in order to restore the economy; unfortunately, by what is now regarded as a slip of the tongue on the hustings, Ward gave an undertaking to borrow, not seven, but £70 million. Who could resist that? The result was that the Reform Government and the United Party won twenty-eight seats each; and the United Party could count on Labour's nineteen members to support them against the conservatives. Ward died in 1930, but by then the Liberal rump was teetering toward coalition with the Reform members. In the 1931 elections, the new coalition won fifty-one of the seats, giving it a triumphant majority.

The Depression, however, was its undoing. In 1935, Labour won with fifty-five seats (including two non-Labour Maori members who joined the Government team). The United-Reform group had contested that poll as the National Political Federation, and the next year they became the New Zealand National Party, regaining the Treasury benches in 1949, and being dislodged only between 1957 and 1960, and 1972 and 1975. The Labour Party has remained substantially the same since its formation in 1916, although in recent years there have been suggestions that it change its title to Social Democratic.

Third parties have never succeeded, apart from Labour, which by its growth soon restored the two-party system. The most enduring in recent decades has been Social Credit, a party of monetary reform. The Social Creditors influenced many of the early Labour leaders, but found that they were discarded after Labour won office. The movement lay dormant through the war years, then sprang back at the 1954 elections taking 11 per cent of the votes. But they were unable to make any breakthrough in that poll, nor in the 1957, 1960 and 1963 elections. In 1966, Social Credit at last won a seat, just to lose it again in 1969. Then they languished again until winning a by-election in 1978, another in 1980, retaining both seats in the 1981 general election.

One matter which preoccupies all New Zealand politicians, regardless of their party, is the management of the national economy. In recent years the economy has been in trouble caused by increasing prices for imported fuels while exports were not able to compensate. The answer has been to massively increase the public debt, both internally and externally, not, as Vogel intended, necessarily to expand the economy, but rather to maintain the internal standard of living. It was the oil shocks of the early 1970s which forced the Rowling Labour Government of the day to start massive borrowing abroad, so that overseas debt has been representing an increasing proportion of total State indebtedness. In the 1979-1980 financial year there was a net increase of $647 million in foreign debt, $879 million in internal debt.

The preoccupation of the recent governments is the coupling of the Overseas Trade and Foreign Affairs portfolio in the hands of the same minister, with Trade being pre-eminent. New Zealand's foreign policy is trade, a position that was voiced by Prime Minister Muldoon a few years ago. Because of the lack of oil and mineral deposits (apart from bountiful supplies of coal), New Zealand is largely dependent on imported raw materials to keep its economy going, although the search for fuel is dealt with in detail below. More than 85 per cent of its imports are raw materials. To pay for this, New Zealand is constantly seeking new markets abroad for its agricultural exports which comprised (with timber) 64 per cent of the goods shipped abroad as at 1980.

The scope of New Zealand's agricultural industries is clearly illustrated by contrasting the population of just over 3 million, with the 62 million sheep, 5.5 million beef cattle, 3 million dairy cattle, 0.5 million pigs and poultry numbering over 3 million. There are 14 million hectares of grasslands, 0.5 million hectares of crops and fruit and 0.75 million hectares of exotic forest. There are 56,000 farms and 12,000 orchards or other horticultural operations. The effect of Britain entering the European Economic Community in 1973 was shattering. Britain had traditionally been an open market for New Zealand farmers who were able to undercut most other producers even after transporting their produce 20,000 kilometres. Since 1973, New Zealand has fought hard and long to maintain as much of the British market as it can, knowing that the farmers of France and other EEC countries want the United Kingdom market for themselves. Between 1965 and 1981 New Zealand's exports to Europe have been declining: in 1965, 67 per cent of the nation's exports went to countries now in the EEC; in 1980, only 30 per cent were sold to the same area.

Many new markets have been found, and never again will New Zealand allow itself to be too heavily dependent on one market. In the early 1970s, New Zealand made its first foray into the Latin American markets, selling huge amounts of milk powder in Chile and Peru. Now New Zealand milk powder is exported to many countries, with Peru alone taking $12 million worth in 1980, with the Philippines, Indonesia and Malaysia being other large customers. Japan and the United States have become increasingly large buyers of lamb, as has the Middle East. Timber and paper products are shipped in huge quantities to Australia, China, Japan, Hong Kong and South Korea. Industrial exports have grown in quantity, but the New Zealand economy is still largely reliant on its farms.

The nation's primary exports, meat, wool, butter and cheese, have been kept competitive in price largely through the mechanisation of agriculture and the climate which allows the animals to feed off pasture all year round. Farms employ little outside

An early coaling station in the Bay of Islands, c. 1888. Coal was in great demand in the nineteenth century and was supplied from townships such as Kawakawa, Whau-whau and Kamo. With massive increases in the cost of imported fuel in the 1970s and 1980s, coal is expected to regain its previous importance and it is anticipated that production will double in the next ten years.

Harvesting on the Taiera Plains last century. These fertile plains, some ten kilometres out of Dunedin, were a scene of great activity during the harvesting season. Today there are half a million hectares of crops and fruit in New Zealand. The leading cash crops are wheat, oats, barley, maize, peas, potatoes and linseed.

labour; the farmer does the bulk of the tasks, the rest of the family being called in at particularly busy times. The hill country runs employ musterers, and some farms are run by salaried managers, but these are in the minority. On the average farm, the only outside hired labour will be for specific tasks the owner cannot manage, such as sheep shearing, or harvesting, for which contractors with heavy equipment are required.

Shearers are some of the more colourful characters in New Zealand farming. They work in gangs which provide the farmer with a total service, from those who can sometimes clip more than 200 sheep a day, and the workers who bale and press the wool, to those who sweep the floor of the shearing shed. Sheep are found in every farming region of New Zealand, and farms range from the hill country stations with 10,000 or more sheep to the small farms on the lusher lowlands which are used to fatten stock. The high country runs concentrate on wool, while the lowland farms produce the lamb and mutton. There are numerous types of sheep, although the Romney is the staple animal which produces a crossbred coarse wool. Farms in the more fertile areas can diversify considerably. A relatively small holding on the Taieri Plain, just outside Dunedin, can produce a comfortable income by producing both wool and meat from its flock, planting a paddock or two in wheat or potatoes, another in lucerne which can supply additional winter feed for the farm and an income from the sale of the surplus. When wool prices dipped sharply in the mid 1960s, many farmers switched to beef cattle but the balance is still sharply in favour of sheep – they produce not only meat but wool.

Dairying was made possible, as was shown in a previous chapter, by the advent of refrigeration. It grew slowly at first because the new settlers did not know much about dairy farming, but by 1900 more than £1 million worth of butter and cheese were exported for the first time. Dairy farms tend to be small in land area, and because the cows require good pasture all year round, the main dairying areas are located in the North Island districts that have good rainfall. It is probably the most onerous form of farming, where the dairy farmer has to rise without fail before dawn and get his cows into the shed. Once the milk was left at the farm gate in churns, but now it is pumped into huge articulated trucks with stainless steel tankers. Most of the stock is drawn from Friesian and Jersey breeds, averaging two and a half beasts to the hectare. Production is impressive by world standards – each cow accounting for 130 kilograms of milkfat a year. Like most other farming, dairying is highly mechanised, with some sheds being capable of processing 350 cows in an hour. In 1980, the dairy industry's production totalled more than $700 million in value.

Cropping provides a huge variety of cereals, vegetables and fruit, both to fulfil New Zealand's own needs and to provide valuable exports. The leading cash crops are wheat, oats, barley, maize, peas, potatoes and linseed. Canterbury is the nation's leading crop area, producing more than half the annual wheat yield, although there has been a trend in recent years for more wheat and barley crops to be planted in the North Island. Peas are grown in Marlborough and Wellington as well as Canterbury, while potato production is centred near Auckland, in the Manawatu and in Canterbury (although the Otago Peninsula, near Dunedin, grows a particularly fine potato which sells at extremely high prices at the beginning of the season). Nearly 90 million hectares are planted in wheat.

Market gardens produce a wide range of vegetables, although many are not readily available all year round. In volume terms, the major vegetable crops are cabbage, carrots, cauliflower, lettuce and tomatoes in the fresh vegetable market, but for the food-processing industry beans, peas and sweet corn dominate. Fruit orchards produce apples, apricots, oranges, avocado, kiwifruit, pears and many others. Many of the specialist crops are exported, particularly to Australia to fill seasonal gaps there, while the kiwifruit, a sweet, green, fleshy fruit with a furry brown skin, has become a major horticultural export, and the market is growing quickly.

Forestry is part of both the primary and secondary industry fields, and must be considered one of the real success stories of the past few decades. The catastrophic wholesale destruction of the native forests has been well documented, and the question of milling indigenous trees continues to be controversial, both on a national level when recently the New Zealand Forest Service proposed to exploit the South Island beech forests, and locally when the matter becomes a choice between keeping a stand of native timber or allowing a sawmilling operation to stay in business and provide employment in a small community.

Exotic forests, on the other hand, were planted to be cut down, and annual planting continues at a rate of about 45,000 hectares a year, and in the next decade will lay the groundwork for a huge expansion in timber production. Already forestry provides work for more than 10 per cent of New Zealanders engaged in manufacturing. Many of those people live in the new towns of the North Island which grew along with the forests – towns like Tokoroa which has about 20,000 people, or Kawerau. Tokoroa serves the New Zealand Forest Products mill at Kinleith, while the Tasman Pulp and Paper Company is located at Kawerau in the Bay of Plenty.

Less of a success story is the fishing industry. New Zealand now has one of the largest economic management zones in the world, but has exploited the sea with little enthusiasm. By and large the fishing fleet is made up of small boats, leaving the organised large-scale fishing to foreign vessels. Control in the past over these fleets has not been made easier by a totally inadequate naval presence. Three-quarters of New Zealand fishing boats are under nine metres in length, while the USSR, South Korea and Japan have been licensed to operate in the Exclusive Economic Zone of more than a million square nautical miles.

New Zealand's manufacturing sector has had a chequered past, at times protected from foreign competition, at others exposed to

In the latter half of the nineteenth century timber was the most promising industry in New Zealand after wool and mutton. The most frequently used trees were the kauri, totara manuka and black birch, and saw mills were plentiful. Today, forestry provides work for more than 10 per cent of New Zealanders engaged in manufacturing. Huge expansion is taking place in the timber industry and annual planting is at a rate of around 45,000 hectares a year.

the chill blast of imports. In 1938, Labour introduced import licensing which was designed to save overseas funds and to encourage New Zealand manufacturing. It was – and is – a system which allows considerable distortions, and has been blamed for fostering inefficient industries. It also needs an army of public servants to administer. Labour re-imposed import controls when they returned to power in 1957. Keith Sinclair, biographer of Prime Minister Walter Nash, quoted one account of the meetings over which Nash presided to work out priorities under the scheme, going into some detail in trying to decide whether working-class families needed more or less quantities of imported tinned salmon and prunes. While the scheme saved the nation's foreign reserves and helped generate new jobs, it also accustomed the public to strange market forces. A notorious example was the import of motor cars.

Visitors to New Zealand in the 1950s and 1960s were struck by the legions of aging automobiles on the roads. Old Austins, Morris's and Vauxhalls which had long disappeared from British roads were highly valued around the other side of the world. Such were the controls on car imports that those citizens who had funds overseas had priority for new cars because they could pay some of the cost from those funds. The rest of the population was consigned to putting their names on waiting lists that stretched into months and years. Those lucky enough to be able to buy a new car off the floor with foreign funds could re-sell the vehicle at a later date for little less than they paid for it originally, and even cars ten or more years old commanded amazingly high prices.

Light industries producing consumer goods have flourished – carpets and textiles, refrigerators and washing machines, footwear, clothing and processed food are among the success stories, and these industries have managed to penetrate the Australian market which provides a potential buying public nearly five times the size of the home market. The New Zealand-Australia Free Trade Agreement has been gradually widened to include more and more products over the years, and this fosters interdependence between the two former British colonies. The proposed closer economic relationship will draw the two economies more tightly together, and help solve the traditional problem for any factory in New Zealand – that the country simply does not have enough customers to provide economies of scale.

But the major problem New Zealand is facing up to is how to reduce dependence on imported fuel now that the halcyon days of cheap oil have well and truly gone. The country has been fortunate to have rivers which have allowed the development of hydroelectric power stations; unlike Europe, there has never been any need in the past for the massive coal-fired power stations and installations like the Meremere coal power station are an exception. All the major rivers – the Waikato, Waitaki, Clutha – have been harnessed. The largest hydro station is at Lake Manapouri, but most of that has gone to the Bluff aluminium smelter. The big problem is that most of the exploitable rivers – the lower Clutha, lower Waitaki and the Buller – are in the South Island, while the main demand is in the northern half of the North Island. A submarine cable below Cook Strait already conducts power to the North, but another would be needed if all these rivers were fully tapped. The other problem is that much development arouses strong opposition. In 1972, one of the major factors which defeated the National Government was its proposal to raise Lake Manapouri for further hydro output; the building of a new dam on the Clutha has been carried out over furious opposition in Otago, while the Motu River in the North Island now has a protection order covering more than sixty kilometres of its course.

The same forces which make mud bubble at Rotorua can also provide harnessed energy. Geothermal power provides industrial steam and electricity for the Tasman Pulp and Paper Mill at Kawerau. It powers the Wairakei power station, and another geothermal station is in the process of being built there.

For more than a decade natural gas has been supplied from Kapuni in Taranaki and reticulated by pipeline to major North Island cities for use in homes and factories, while the offshore Maui gasfield supplies the New Plymouth power station. The gas pipelines are now being extended to link Northland and Hawke's Bay. Over the next fifteen years the New Zealand Government will be involved in major fuel projects, including coal, electricity and liquid fuels. In the next ten years coal production is expected to double. By 1995, four new stations will be in service using coal as fuel, the largest being at Huntly in the Waikato which consumes 2 million tonnes of coal a year. These major new mines in the Waikato will provide coal for power stations – which will now be needed as the cheaper hydro options have been exhausted – and for a steel mill. The old Meremere station will be upgraded and will operate until the new stations come into service. Continuous mining machines are now being used in some of the larger opencast fields, while the coal deposits on the West Coast are set down for further development to step up export of coal to Japan and South Korea. Both Central Otago and Southland contain massive deposits of lignite coal which have been confirmed only in recent years – but their exploitation would mean ripping up huge areas of farming land, which may not be acceptable.

Exciting prospects lie in front of the gas industry, including a chemical methanol plant and a synthetic petrol plant. Nearly 2000 vehicles in New Zealand are being converted every month to compressed natural gas with the plan that 10 per cent of vehicles will be using CNG by 1990. The synthetic petrol plant at Motonui will make petrol from the natural gas.

Some of these schemes are under way. Others are still on the planning board. And, given the ability of governments to change, some might never come to fruition. Meanwhile, the search for oil continues around New Zealand's coast. Seismic teams comb the country looking for hopeful signs. Energy is now the key to New Zealand's future. With a major reduction in the need for imported fuels, the country can look forward to a new era of prosperity.